The COLOR *of* LIGHT

Commissioning Stained Glass for a Church

Sarah Hall

LTP

LITURGY
TRAINING
PUBLICATIONS

The Color of Light

ACKNOWLEDGMENTS

I would like to thank Peter Larisey, SJ, Professor Shirley Ann Brown and architectural historian Peter Coffman for generously sharing their expertise on the history chapter. I am also deeply indebted to the many artists who provided images of their exceptional and beautiful work. Finally, I would like to offer special thanks to my husband, Jeffrey Kraegal, for his wisdom, tireless support and collaboration on this book.
Sarah Hall

Visit our website at www.ltp.org.

This book was edited by David Philippart and designed by Peter Pona. Bryan Cones was the production editor. Typesetting was done by Kari Nicholls in Berkeley, Bauer Bodoni and Engravers Gothic. Front cover photo is by Sarah Hall. Frontispiece image is from "Saint Michael at the End of Time" by Sarah Hall. Photo by William Lindsay.

03   02   01   00   99   5   4   3   2   1

Library of Congress Cataloging-in-Publication Data
Hall, Sarah, 1951–
    The color of light: commissioning stained glass for a church /
Sarah Hall.
      p. cm.
    ISBN 1-56854-311-5
    1. Class craft.   2. Glass painting and staining.   I. Title.
TT298.H33   1999
748.5—dc21   99-27786
                                       CIP

COLOR

TABLE OF CONTENTS

THIS BOOK WAS WRITTEN TO HONOR
THE BEAUTY OF GLASS, TO RECOGNIZE THE
TRANSFORMATIONAL ROLE IT CAN PLAY IN
A CHURCH BUILDING, AND TO HELP PARISHES,
ARCHITECTS AND CLERGY TO COMMISSION
BEAUTIFUL AND MEANINGFUL STAINED GLASS
FOR PLACES OF WORSHIP.

Introduction

The use of colored glass to ornament church windows dates back at least fifteen hundred years, and leaded stained glass as we know it at least a thousand. The exact origin of this ancient art is unknown, but the reason for its continuing popularity is no mystery — stained glass, with its ability to alter and shape light, transforms interior spaces in a way that no other art form can.

The addition of stained glass to a church is an exciting event, and those involved in the commissioning process have a wonderful opportunity to bring greater beauty and deeper meaning to their church building. The task may seem daunting — especially for someone new to the process. Being an admirer of stained glass does not necessarily prepare one for all that is involved in planning and managing the creation of a stained glass window or series of windows. Nevertheless, those commissioning stained glass can, with the information in this book, choose an artist, commission beautiful windows, and manage the process to its successful completion.

The purpose of this book is to demystify the process of working with stained glass artists and to establish a format for the commissioning process. It seeks to be a guide for client and artist alike that will encourage more deeply considered, integrated and expressive artwork in our places of worship.

A note about this book: Italicized words indicate a term that can be found in the glossary, beginning on page 96.

Figure 1. Mediating light, stained glass invites awe. Photo by Sarah Hall.

WHAT IS A STAINED GLASS WINDOW?

A careful look at a stained glass window reveals a fairly simple structure. If the window was made in the traditional leaded technique, then it was put together from pieces of colored *glass*, cut to shape and perhaps treated, and then arranged in a pattern. The individual pieces were set in place with a lattice of H-shaped *lead* strips, or *cames*, that were *soldered* at the joints. The panel was then installed in a window opening and became part of the building.

Good craftsmanship is essential in the creation of stained glass. The care taken in the planning, design, selection of materials, fabrication and installation of a window makes all the difference in how it looks when it is new, as well as when it is ten, fifty, or a hundred years old.

But a window's success depends on far more than just the level of craftsmanship, important as that is. Stained glass in a church exists within a web of connections — physical, architectural, historical, theological and social — that transcends the simple structure of the window itself. It is these connections that give a window meaning and context, and place it within the assembly of God's people. These connections also make the commissioning process interesting and exciting, for a window that works well within its context has a richness that will touch the spirit of everyone who worships in or visits the church.

In light of this, the answer to the question, "What is a stained glass window?" is clearly twofold. First, a stained glass window is an arrangement of treated glass pieces in a lead matrix. Second, and more importantly, a stained glass window is a lasting and integral part of a church building, and is inspired by and connected to a vast web of people, events and spiritual aspirations, past, present and future.

This book is a guide to understanding both parts of the answer, a way of seeing through both sides of the window.

Figure 2. Glassblower at Glashütte Lamberts, Waldsassen, Germany, making handblown antique glass. Photo by Sarah Hall.

MATERIALS

Glass is a remarkable material. Its roots lie in the plainest of materials, sand. When heated to a molten, glowing liquid, it seems to ignite with the first light of its new form. As it cools on the end of the glassmaker's blowpipe, it takes on a taffy-like consistency and can be stretched, shaped, cut, bent and flattened with metal tools. Once cool, the glowing material becomes rigid and transparent. It can now be cut and treated for use in the fashioning of a stained glass window.

Although it is temperamental, fragile and unforgiving in the studio, once glass is leaded and installed in a window, it becomes one of the most durable of materials. Even after hundreds of years, stained glass remains a living substance, expanding and contracting with the days and the seasons.

People have been making glass for thousands of years, and the processes modern glassmakers use have evolved over the course of time. This evolution has resulted in improved efficiency and consistency, culminating in the clear, perfectly even modern *float glass*. While a technological marvel, modern glass is not very interesting to look at; it is mostly looked *through*. Not surprisingly, glass artists gravitate toward materials made with older methods, and the textures, imperfections and incomparable colors that they bring. These bubbles, striations and uneven surfaces have the effect of trapping light in the glass, giving it a greater luminosity and shimmer.

There are several techniques for producing handmade stained glass. In the most common technique, the glassblower begins by gathering a knob of molten glass on the end of a blowpipe. This knob, or "gather," is blown and shaped into a long, hollow cylinder (figure 2). The glassblower, working with an experienced team, removes the ends of the cylinder, and the resulting "muff" is allowed to cool. The cylinder is then scored along its length and reheated in a *lehr,* a long oven, which allows it to open up and flatten into a sheet that is then smoothed by a wooden block. The sheet is then *annealed,* cooled very slowly and evenly, to relieve the stresses in it.

Many techniques are used to enhance the beauty and character of the glass both during and after this process. Color is produced through the dissolution of metal oxides, sulfides and other substances into the molten glass. Other colorants may be dispersed as microscopic particles. The specific coloring process used can make a significant difference in the cost of the glass. Fine particles of gold are sometimes used in making gold-ruby or gold-pink glass; the price reflects the use of this precious ingredient.

The coloring process results in glass that is rich in color and texture, with a wonderfully lively interior life. A close look at a piece of handmade stained glass opens up a new world: Each piece tells the story of how it was made — from its origin in sand and metal oxides, to the blasting heat of the glass kiln, to the pressing and shaping that turned a blob of molten glass into a sheet of frozen color.

As glass is made it can be textured, layered, striated and molded to achieve some lovely effects. Some of the available kinds of *antique glass* are described below. (The word "antique" refers to the process by which the glass is made, not the age of the glass.)

Streaky glass is made by mixing different colors of glass in the furnace. The resulting swirls and patterns can range from subtle changes in one color to riotous streaks of many colors within one sheet of glass.

Because it is so visually active, artists use streaky glass with care (figure 3).

Reamy glass is made in a way similar to streaky, but instead of mixing colors, glasses of varying hardnesses are mixed. The glass that results has a surface roiled with waves and ripples, much like the frozen surface of a pond. Because of the varying thickness in a single piece, reamy glass can be tricky to cut. Care must be taken in the orientation of the glass as well, so that the "flow" of the texture is maintained from one piece to the next (figure 6).

Flashed glass is created by dipping a hot gather of molten glass into another color. The result is a thin layer of color on the original base glass. Depending on how this is done, the color can change or almost disappear across the surface of the glass.

The most common type of flashed glass consists of a layer of color over a transparent base. An infinite number of other effects can be achieved by changing both the color of the flash and the color of the base glass. *Opak* is created by flashing white onto colored antique. As the name suggests, the result is nearly opaque. *Opal* glass appears as a translucent skin of light—a pearl-like finish flashed

(Above) Figure 3. Jürgen Reipka used multi-colored streaky glass in this panel detail. This work is also painted. Photo by Sarah Hall.

(Right) Figure 4. Glass on the easel at the Sattler Studio. Photo by Helga Sattler.

onto clear or colored glass. Used as a design element, opak or opal glass can provide privacy in interior settings. In exterior windows, these glasses seem to catch and hold the light, while at the same time keeping the color from flooding the interior. Colors are flashed onto a variety of base colors: white, yellow, pink, blue, gray and even green.

Artists use two important techniques to achieve certain effects with flashed glass. In one technique, the flashed side is covered with a masking material, and a pattern is cut into the material. The piece is then *acid-etched* or *sandblasted* to remove the flash, leaving a pattern in the color of the base glass.

Another technique uses the natural variations in the flash itself to create the desired pattern or image. By carefully choosing the sheets and keeping the design in mind when cutting, an artist can use the natural patterns and shapes in flashed glass to achieve a painterly quality without using paint.

Seedy glass contains thousands of tiny air bubbles distributed throughout the glass. The bubbles can be made in a number of ways. One method is to pull the glass from the furnace before the air bubbles have been refined by time and heat. Another, more interesting way to produce bubbles is to toss a vegetable, for example a potato, into the molten glass. The tossed item is vaporized, and the chemical reaction between its elements and the glass produces air bubbles. Seedy glass has a distinctive look and brings texture, movement and variety to the window. The bubbles shine like jewels in the sunlight and are constantly transformed with the changing light of the day.

Crown glass is made by spinning a glass bubble on the end of a rod and cutting open one end to allow the bubble to open into a large circular sheet, or *rondel*. The central knob, where the rod was attached, has a characteristic "bull's-eye" appearance. Casting methods are also used to mass-produce modern versions of crown rondels and bull's-eyes.

Bevels, jewels, *prisms* and *lenses* are made by pressing or casting molten glass (either clear or colored) into a mold. These three-dimensional glass objects, which were introduced into stained glass in the Victorian

Figure 5. The central glass in this window by Sarah Hall is a sheet of streaky red on white. Photo by William Lindsay.

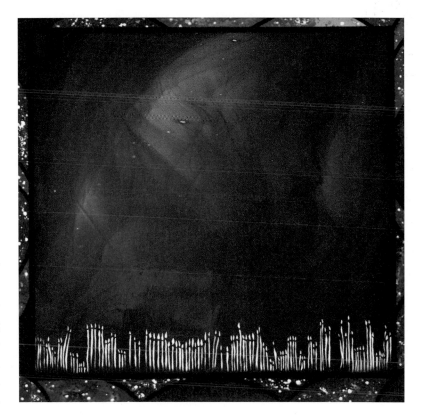

period, have made a comeback today and provide an additional level of animation, texture and sculptural quality to a window (figure 9).

Although incomparably beautiful, handmade glass is also quite expensive. Supply houses balance this by offering mass-produced, colored glass, which is considerably less expensive and more widely available. These machine-made products can be produced in larger sheets than the handmade variety, although they can't equal the textural variety and depth of color of traditional handmade glass.

The most common type of machine-made glass is *cathedral glass*, which is made by flattening molten glass with textured rollers. Cathedral glass is even in color and thickness, and usually has a textured surface, produced by the rollers. It is popular in restaurants, bars and other commercial locations where "stained glass" is desired at a minimal cost. Cathedral glass has also been widely used for domestic windows (*transoms*, door panels, and so forth) and in church windows done in the "rectangles-of-amber-and-blue-style" popular in the 1960s. The even,

Figure 6. Ludwig Schaffrath

made use of reamy clear glass that

has a flowing, icy appearance.

Photo by Sarah Hall.

characterless color of cathedral glass provided a background for the heavily painted windows done in the Victorian Revival style.

American opalescent, used extensively in Tiffany-style windows and lamps, is another machine-made glass. Louis Comfort Tiffany himself created sculpted glass sheets of intriguing beauty and depth. Some contemporary manufacturers are working to recreate this unique glass (figure 10).

Semi-antique glass, which is also called "drawn" or "new" antique glass, mimics the look of *handblown glass* while providing a relatively consistent medium for the craftsperson. It is more interesting than cathedral glass, and its lower cost and wide availability make it suitable for a variety of applications. However, its consistency — while handy for the craftsperson who is cutting and leading it — also robs it of character. The restricted palette of colors also limits the usefulness of this glass.

Next to design, the materials that go into a stained glass window are the most important factor in its success. The design may look great on paper, but the window will only work if the right materials are chosen. In creating a window, the artist considers the color, texture and character of each piece, and thinks about how it will look once it has been painted, *etched,* sandblasted or *silver stained.*

Figure 7. The central circle in this detail of a window by Sarah Hall/Sattler Studio shows a flashed glass with color changes from red to blue. This glass is also screen-painted. Photo by André Beneteau.

Figure 8. A combination of blue opal glass, bevels and dichroic glass were used by David Wilson at Mary Mother of the Church Chapel in Washington, D.C. Photo by David Wilson.

Each piece must also work with its neighbors — the elements that will surround it.

Glass artists are passionate about their materials. Some will use only handblown antique glass; others may want the uniformity of semi-antique. Still others will mix types of glass, using them for contrast or variety throughout the window.

For a committee charged with commissioning a stained glass window, it is important to know the difference between hand- and machine-made glass, and to have some familiarity with the different types of glass available. Artists will often be happy to provide samples of the glasses they will be using. The stained glass in other churches may also allow a comparison of the different types of glass and how they might work in a church building.

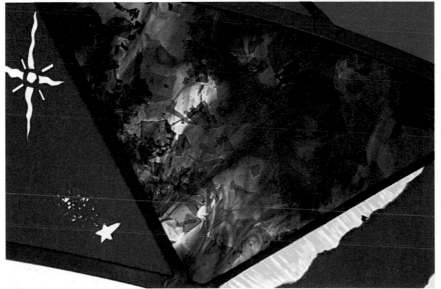

(Above) Figure 9. Jim Piercey used cast glass prisms of different sizes, along with opal blue, at St. Peter the Apostle Catholic Church in Naples, Florida. Photo by Jim Piercey.

(Left) Figure 10. Multi-colored hand-rolled glass in the Tiffany style made by Schlitz Glassworks in Milwaukee, Wisconsin. Photo by Sarah Hall.

Figure 11. Dalle de verre glass wall for the baptistry at the Church of the Sacred Heart, Audincourt, France, designed by artist Fernand Leger. Photo by Sarah Hall.

The Creation of a Stained Glass Window

In an age of mass production, stained glass stands out as an architectural art in which each window is individually made by hand for a specific site. The techniques used today, from design to final installation, are not that different from those of medieval times. As a site-specific art form, stained glass provides artists and congregations with a unique opportunity to shape the window's design to the church building, the assembly and the liturgy.

Design

The creation of a church window begins long before the first piece of glass is cut with the *design*. When creating a design, the artist takes into account many factors: the architecture of the building, the light, the surrounding materials and colors, the needs of the liturgy and themes to be expressed, the concerns of the parish, the budget, and the integration of the new window with the other windows in the building. A good design is the foundation of a successful window.

It is not uncommon for committees to ask an artist for a quick design sketch to get an idea of what the artist may create. While this request is understandable, most professionals will politely refuse for the simple reason that a quick sketch will not look like a window and, furthermore, won't do justice to the many considerations that go into a well-made design. The following process, while requiring more time, will result in a much better design — and a window that will suit the church building and its congregation.

Although each glass artist goes about designing a window in different ways, he or she will typically begin with several ideas and then work through them until they are narrowed down to the two or three strongest.

The artist will then develop these ideas over a period of days or weeks until the design feels "right" for the building and the assembly. Some artists create architectural models as part of their design work (figures 12 and 13). This is especially helpful when an entire set of windows is being designed for a new church. Photographs of the window's location in the building and of the surrounding structures are valuable for reference throughout the design process. In all, the design process may involve dozens of preliminary drawings. The artist then presents the proposed design and works with the commissioning committee to finalize it.

A well-designed window should first of all fit the building; it should give a sense of being a natural and integral part of the church rather than a tacked-on afterthought. This involves many factors, including the architectural style, colors appropriate to the site, and the direction and intensity of the light at different times of day and in different seasons. Light is life to a stained glass window, and how the window uses the light in its environment will make the difference between a piece that "breathes" and glows with color, and one that disappears into shadows and reflections.

During the design process, then, it is essential to observe the window's surroundings — to "listen" to the building and to respond with an artwork that is right for the space. It is important to remember that the life span of a building, a window or even a parish is not the same as that of a single human being. A stained glass window will remain long after its creators have passed on. If only for this reason, a window must be right for its surroundings.

(Right) Figure 12. The design

process often begins with an

architectural model. Photo

by William Lindsay.

(Below) Figure 13. Scale model

and sketch for "Radiance,

Reflection, Revelation."

Figures 13–24 show the process of making "Radiance, Reflection,

Revelation," a glass tower 50 feet high by 12 feet wide. Designed

and made by Sarah Hall Studio, this window portrays the church

as a spiritual center for the assembly. Located in the First Unitarian

Congregation in Toronto, Canada, the design was inspired by the

Unitarian symbol of the flaming chalice. The column uses highly-

textured, prismatic and beveled clear glass to form a sinuous

golden spiral. The images illustrate the leaded technique used

by Sarah Hall Studio. Photos courtesy of Sarah Hall Studio.

The window should also mesh with the personality and spirit of the parish, those who will live and worship with the window in this generation and those to come. And of course, like any piece of art in a church building, the window needs to serve the actions of the liturgy, so that it creates a fitting place for the sacred rites. Careful design makes all the difference between a successful stained glass window and a mere "decoration."

Another important element of any window is its historical context. Every stained glass window relates to the history of the art, whether it is inspired by previous windows, is a reaction against past styles or aesthetics, or simply tries to imitate older works. It is impossible to set clear guidelines on how a window should relate to a historical context; suffice it to say that a window should contribute to the dialogue, advancing the conversation, not just repeating what has been said before.

The final design itself will depend on the artist. Artists have different techniques for creating window designs — some very open-ended and casual, others with every line figured out. The most important thing for the client to remember is that the presented design is just a sketch, not a miniature window. A design on paper cannot capture the glow and transparency of stained glass. There is a leap of the imagination that the client must make to visualize the window. Only stained glass looks like stained glass; this is one of the main reasons for its continued popularity!

FABRICATION

After the committee approves the design, the fabrication of the window begins. Each of the steps described below is part of a process designed to produce a strong, stable, weatherproof stained glass window. Although window production is most clearly the "craft" of stained glass, the artist has an important role throughout the process, including making decisions and taking part in certain steps, in order to make sure that the artistic intent of the window comes through in the final product.

Figure 14. Full-size drawings on the cartoon wall at the studio.

Glass Selection

Color and texture are critical elements in the creation of a window. Both the type of glass and the range of colors are considered in the design process, as even the best design can be ruined by cheap or inappropriate glass. Antique glass, which has the broadest range of colors, is not as easily available as inexpensive cathedral glass, and some time may be needed for it to be ordered or specially made by glass-blowers. It is a good idea to leave adequate time for the desired glass to be obtained.

Cartoon

The *cartoon* is the full-size drawing from which the window is produced. While preliminary sketches can vary from vague and open-ended to precise and specific, ambiguity usually gives way to accuracy in the creation of the cartoon. The cartoon is made to the exact dimensions of the window opening and contains all of the information for details such as painting, etching, sand-blasting, and so forth. Cartoons may be black-and-white or colored, and may also indicate lead sizes and types of glass.

(Above) Figure 15. Cutting the glass.

Each piece is cut and shaped by hand.

(Right) Figure 16. Glass is attached

to the easel with wax to judge the

color relationships in daylight.

(Facing page, top) Figure 17.

The individual panels are leaded.

The detail shows horseshoe nails

that hold the pieces in place

during the glazing.

(Facing page, bottom) Figure 18.

Mixing the cement.

Cutline or Pattern-making

In the cartoon, the size and shape of each piece of glass in the window is planned out. When the time comes for cutting the glass, an accurate guide is needed to make sure each piece will fit perfectly with its neighbors. This guide can take one of two forms. A *cutline* is created by placing tracing paper on top of the cartoon and tracing the heart of each lead-line onto the paper. Alternatively, a paper *template* for each piece can be made. This is done by placing carbon paper under the cartoon and tracing over each of the lines drawn. The paper *pattern* of each piece is then numbered and cut to shape along the carbon paper line.

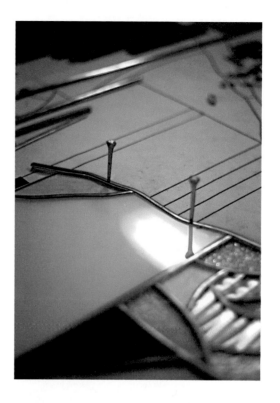

Cutting

Glass cutting is a skill that takes considerable time to develop, especially for intricate, difficult shapes. Cutting is usually done with a small hand tool that scores the glass with a steel wheel. The glass is then separated along the score line. If the *glazier* is using a pattern, he or she places the paper template on top of the glass and then cuts out the shape. With a cutline, the tracing paper is placed underneath the glass to be cut, and the cutter follows the line seen through the glass. After cutting, glass edges are softened with a small hand grindstone or file. *Grozing* pliers can be used to break away bits of glass and perfect the shape. Finally, the pieces of glass can either go directly onto a glass easel or be set into trays to await further treatment.

Treatments

Depending on the design, there may be a great deal of further work to be done on the individual pieces of glass. Among the glass treatments that may be used are painting, acid-etching, sandblasting, enameling, *fusing* and silver staining. Each of these treatments changes the appearance of the glass in a particular way, and they are used to create the different effects required by the design. Glass treatments can be used to add lines, shapes, figures or visual effects to the glass. They can also change or mute the color of the glass in various ways.

Glass treatments are labor intensive and require special equipment. For many techniques, special skills are also needed. Often, a piece of glass requires a combination of treatments and must be fired in a kiln several times. The time involved in painting, staining and *firing* a piece of glass may be triple that of a plain-glazed window (that is, colored glass without further treatments).

The cost is accordingly higher. These glass treatments are further discussed in the next chapter, "Special Effects."

Easel and Waxing-up

Before, during or after various treatments, the glass is usually moved from a flat worktable to a glass easel so that it can be judged in daylight. The configuration of lead-lines is painted onto the easel with black tempera paint in order to give a better idea of what the window will look like. The individual pieces of glass are held in place temporarily on the easel with wax or plastiscine. Changes are made during this time until the artist is satisfied that the glasswork looks as it was intended to.

Glazing

Once all of the pieces of glass are ready, the window is leaded up. The lead came is stretched and opened with a *lathekin*. The flexible H-channel cames are shaped around each piece of glass and cut so that the joints meet perfectly. As the *panel* is being

(Above) Figure 19. Cement is brushed into the lead. The panel is later cleaned with sawdust.
(Right) Figure 20. Final cleanings are made in daylight.

Figure 21. Leaded panels are installed with custom framing, which provides for ventilation between the stained glass and the thermopane exterior.

built, the glass is held in place with horseshoe nails. Each window is put together on a workbench until all of the pieces are in place. The joints are then fluxed to assure good solder adhesion, and the soldering is done on the top side of the panel. The panel is turned over and the other side is soldered. Panels greater than 12 square feet are too flexible and unwieldy for safe handling; this is one reason why large windows are made up of several separate panels.

Cementing

The process of cementing weatherproofs and strengthens the leaded panel, achieving an aesthetic merging of the glass and leads that darkens the leads in the process. The cement, also called putty, that is brushed into the leads is a mixture of plaster, linseed oil, turpentine and a coloring agent. *(continued on page 21)*

(Previous spread) Figure 22.
Two individual leaded panels
incorporate several types of glass:
white opal, amber antique,
iridescent and clear textures,
bevels and dichroic glass.
(Right) Figure 23. "Radiance,
Reflection, Revelation,"
exterior evening view.

Figure 24. Detail of faceted dalle de verre *by Karl Versteeg for a reconciliation room at St. Joan of Arc Church, Toronto, Canada. Photo by Sarah Hall.*

(continued from page 17) After it has been brushed into both sides of the panel, the excess is removed and the glass is further cleaned with sawdust or whiting. The panels are then inspected in daylight, and the leads are polished to bring them to a dark sheen.

INSTALLATION

The installation should be planned well in advance. Panel sizes, framing to hold the windows in place, and scaffold arrangements are part of the stained glass studio's considerations. The panels are packed and shipped to their final destination to be installed. In many new buildings the existing clear thermopane becomes the "protective glazing." For older buildings, the studio generally recommends how best to protect the window. Whatever method is selected, it is essential that the windows are well ventilated to prevent both condensation and build-up of heat between the stained glass and the outside glazing.

DALLE DE VERRE AND OTHER TECHNIQUES

Another major technique in glasswork is known as *dalle de verre*. During the 1940s the French artist Labourette set thick slabs of glass, which were originally manufactured for use as skylights in the Paris subway, in a concrete matrix. His work caught the imagination of many and the technique gained popularity.

Dalle de verre windows are created by casting. Pieces of one-inch-thick *slab glass* (often with faceted edges) are cut to size and arranged in a mold in a designed pattern. Concrete or *epoxy resin* is poured around the pieces of glass. The frame is detached when the concrete or resin is set, usually after three or four days. Both concrete and resin can be colored, and they are generally dusted with sand or a metallic finish to achieve a textured effect. The appearance of *dalle de*

Figure 25.

Artist Tony Lee stands

before his glass screen.

Photo by Sarah Hall.

verre is far more robust and sculptural than leaded stained glass, and the design has a more abstract quality due to the fact that the glass is unpainted and divided by thick, dark lines of concrete or resin. As a result, this technique is well suited to organically shaped church buildings constructed of rugged materials (figure 24).

Additional casting techniques involve glass "blocks" designed by artists. While not standard, these techniques can provide a durable and exceptionally beautiful glass wall or interior screen. The interior glass screen by artist Tony Lee (figures 25 and 26) was created from hot glass forms that were sectioned on a lapidary saw. The sections were then re-formed into kiln-cast inch-thick glass blocks and set into a lattice framework.

Figure 26. This glass screen by Tony Lee shows an elegant fusing of glass-blown forms. Photo by Sarah Hall.

Figure 27. "Hosanna in the Highest" by Elizabeth Devereaux, St. Elizabeth Ann Seton, Rowland Heights, California. Photo by Elizabeth Devereaux.

Special Effects: Techniques and Treatments for Glass

Stained glass offers a wonderfully rich palette for the artist; it is full of potential. In the supply house, sheets of glass are stacked side by side on their edges, cold and dark in open-ended wooden boxes. But when drawn out, a sheet of glass catches the light and comes to life with color. Bright or subdued, smooth or textured, each sheet is a story told in light.

Why do anything to the glass? Indeed, sometimes it is unnecessary. Untreated glass offers a wealth of possibilities, and many windows are made using only the colors and textures found in the glass itself. In very large works this is often the best option, as treated pieces may be lost in the expanse of glass. Large colored fields of glass usually require antique glass, with its subtle color shadings and possibilities. A large expanse of the primary colors and monotonous texture of machine-made glass can be deadly!

When figures, intricate details or special effects are required, glass treatments are the only option. Although the basic techniques for creating leaded stained glass date back to the medieval era, stained glass has evolved with the times. Technical and artistic developments over the centuries have given today's artist a wide range of techniques to choose from. These include such innovative technologies as fusing, *slumping,* and high-tech glues and epoxies.

In essence the techniques used to enhance glass tend to fall into two categories: They either add or remove something to the surface of the glass; or they shape the piece of glass in a kiln.

Painting

Painting is the oldest form of glass treatment, dating almost to the earliest stained glass of 1000 CE. *Glass paint* is made of finely ground glass combined with black or brown iron oxide in a liquid carrier, which may be water- or oil-based. Pieces of glass are painted and then fired, fusing the paint permanently to the surface of the glass. Since the painted surface is installed on the inside of the window, it will last nearly as long as the glass itself.

Glass painting shades or blocks the light coming through a piece of glass, contrasting with the light shining through the unpainted glass around it. With glass paint, an artist can temper a color, extend a leadline, and create figures, objects and textures. Sometimes an artist uses the paint itself to create an illusion of perspective, thereby creating a sense of varying dimensions within the work. Glass artists also use paint to soften the leaded linework, binding individual pieces of glass into a cohesive tonal element. However it is used, paint on glass tends to focus the eye on the surface, drawing attention away from the exterior view (figures 28 – 33).

Enamels

Colored *enamels* have been used in glass painting since the seventeenth century. Although they cannot match the vibrancy of color found in antique glass, artists are showing renewed interest in enamels because of their subdued effect and suitability for interior settings with natural light (figure 37).

Silver Stain

Another traditional technique is silver stain. This technique, discovered in the fourteenth century, revolutionized the art of stained glass. In contrast to the opacity of paint, silver stain is luminous, *(continued on page 32)*

Figures 28–33. Throughout its long history,

the technique of glass painting has remained

the same. Its style and subject matter,

however, have reflected the changing times.

Figure 28. Painted glass by N. T. Lyons

(ca. 1880). Photo by Sarah Hall.

(Left) Figure 29. Painted glass

by Sister Nicole Oblinger

(ca. 1990). Photo by Sarah Hall.

(Below) Figure 30. Painted glass

by Yvonne Williams (ca. 1940).

Photo by William Lindsay.

(Left) Figure 31. Painted glass by Harry Clarke (ca. 1910).

Photo by Sarah Hall.

(Below) Figure 32. Painted glass by Joachim Klos (ca. 1980).

Photo by Sarah Hall.

Figure 33. Painted glass by

Stephen Taylor (ca. 1970).

Photo by Sarah Hall.

Figures 34–36. Although screen painting on glass was developed during the Victorian period, it has been rediscovered by contemporary artists. Screen painting is used to create both images and graphic textures.

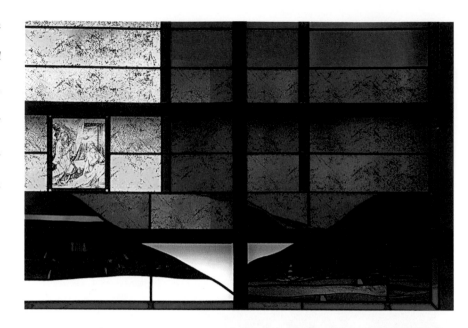

(Left) Figure 37. "Gather Us in the Spirit," Newman Center, Columbia, Missouri, by Elizabeth Deveraux. The use of lusters, air-brushing and enamels provides a softer, more painterly quality than traditional glass-painting.

(Below) Figure 38. Windows in St. Martin Church, Frfurt, Germany, by Tobias Kammerer.

(Opposite page, top) Figure 34. Detail from "Mystery of the Rosary" windows at St. Andrew Church, Columbus, Ohio, by Sarah Hall/Sattler Studio. Photo by Peter Coffman.

(Opposite page, bottom left) Figure 35. Window for the daily chapel at St. Peter's Church, Geneva, Illinois, by Kenneth von Roenn, Jr. Photo courtesy of Kenneth von Roenn, Jr.

(Opposite page, bottom right) Figure 36. Detail from the Crucifixion window at Immaculate Conception Church in Woodbridge, Ontario, by Sarah Hall/Sattler Studio. Photo by André Beneteau.

Figures 39–41. Silver stain,

discovered in the fourteenth century,

has a long, continuous tradition in

stained glass. Painted onto the glass

and fired, it turns the glass pale

yellow to deep amber. Although it is

expensive, many stained glass artists

love this mecurial, unpredictable

coloring agent. Photos by Sarah Hall.

(continued from page 25) catching the sunlight and holding it in the glass. The technique involves the painting of silver nitrate onto the glass, which is then fired in a kiln. The nitrate embeds itself permanently into the glass, resulting in coloration that is pale yellow to deep amber (figures 39–41).

PLATING

A simple additive technique, which has been helped by modern materials, is that of *plating,* or layering. In earlier times, two pieces of glass were sometimes sandwiched, allowing the blended colors to show as one. The development of clear, long-lasting glues allowed glass to be fastened to glass anywhere on a window. This allows for the addition of colored glass, prisms and lenses to the surface of a base glass.

ETCHING

Several techniques available to the glass artist create effects by modifying the glass's surface. Because they work as an extension of a piece of glass, they maintain its original beauty and character. Among these, an early innovation in stained glass treatment was the abrasion, or etching, of the surface of a double-layered (flashed) glass. Because red or "ruby" glass in its full thickness tends to be nearly opaque, early artisans created glass with a thin layer of red "flashed" onto a thicker layer of clear glass. Sometimes, artists would scrape away the flashed layer in places to create areas of clear glass within the red. They began to apply this technique to other colors as well, and today it is an important aspect of the glass artist's craft. More recently, sandblasting and acid-etching with hydrofluoric acid have replaced manual abrasion in the removal of the colored layer.

Acid-etching is a wonderfully versatile technique. It can create bold sweeps of color or achieve subtle graduations of tone. Acid-etching maintains the glass's transparency rather than obscuring it. While painting focuses attention on the surface of the glass, acid-etching draws the eye through the glass, even as it adds shape and texture.

SANDBLASTING

Closely related to etching is sandblasting. Used on clear or colored glass, sandblasting cuts the surface shine of the glass and replaces *(continued on page 36)*

(Opposite page) Figure 39. Silver

stain by Wilhelm Bernhard, Austria.

(Left) Figure 40. Silver stain by

Sarah Hall, Canada.

(Below) Figure 41. Silver stain

by Graham Jones, England.

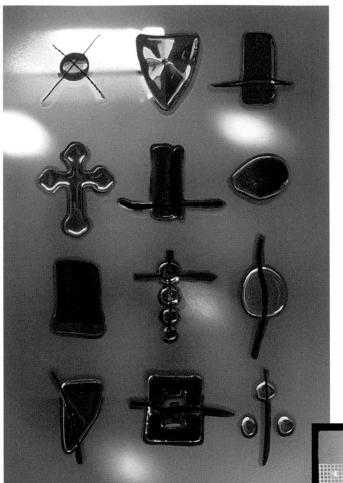

Figure 42. Gordon Huether used a combination of fused glass, sandblasting and clear adhesive to create this work. Photo by Sarah Hall.

Figure 43. This project by Kenneth von Roenn, Jr., for the Abbey of Gethsemani in Kentucky combines sandblasted antique glass (the blue and white) with leaded, bevelled and sandblasted clear glass. The design was developed from traditional Cistercian grisaille patterns. Photo by Kenneth von Roenn, Jr.

(Left) Figure 44. In the day chapel at Mary, Queen of the Universe Shrine in Orlando, Florida, Kenneth von Roenn, Jr., has created a celestial atmosphere with sandblasted flashed glass. The object of this window was to create a quiet, calm environment, conducive to meditation and prayer. Photo by Kenneth von Roenn, Jr.

(Below) Figure 45. In a detail from a window at St. Simon's Anglican Church in Toronto, Canada, Doreen Balabanoff used acid-etching to achieve an exquisite heaven for her "Omnia Opera" theme. Photo by Sarah Hall.

(continued from page 32) it with a soft, diffuse whiteness. If a *resist* is applied prior to sandblasting, the sandblasting will only affect areas where the resist is cut away. This technique can be used to create a pattern, an image or shading. Sandblasting can also be used on thicker glass to sculpt or *carve* the surface.

Sandblasting is usually done in a cabinet that contains pressurized sand or an abrasive aluminum grit. "Etched" refers to lightly sandblasted glass that has a frosted appearance. "Carved" refers to glass with a sculptured, dimensional effect achieved by deep sandblasting executed in various stages or layers. Sandblasted glass is often used for interior screens and settings that receive filtered or artificial light (figures 42–44).

ENGRAVING

Although engraved glass is usually used for smaller objects, it can also be used in windows. Artist John Hutton used handheld, motorized engraving machines to create his masterful glass screen at Coventry Cathedral. The 70-foot transparent glass screen is engraved with magnificent figures of angels, saints and prophets. It looks out onto the charred ruins of the old cathedral, which was destroyed during World War II.

SANDCASTING

Sandcasting is a sculptural technique occasionally used in windows. In a sandcast piece artist Jeff Goodman created a sculptural glass work in which symbolic elements were pressed into soft sand and molten glass poured into the mold. The cooled glass was annealed and framed in a metal *armature*. This "hot glass" technique, along with others such as fusing and kilncasting, offers many beautiful new possibilities for windows, interior screens, entryways, fonts and vessels.

For the person commissioning glass, an understanding of glass-enhancing techniques is useful in the planning of a window. The artist can provide samples of glass that have been treated using the techniques described above. Photographs of previous works can also help. Finally, visiting other churches and looking at how the various techniques have been used can give an idea of how they contribute to a window.

(Opposite page, left) Figure 46. Jürgen Reipka/Sattler Studio has created a window for the chapel of the Andachtsraum Hospital in Langenau, Germany. In his work the techniques of painting and sandblasting take on new proportions and maintain the sharp, strong energy of his paintings on canvas. Photo by Norbert Sattler.

(Opposite page, right) Figure 47. At the Centenary United Methodist Church in Los Angeles, California, Elizabeth Devereaux worked with the Japanese American congregation, portraying its Japanese roots growing into the next generation. Gradation in tone gives a very painterly quality to the window. The circle, symbolizing God and eternity, is intersected by a stylized plum tree that blossoms in the dead of winter. Photo by Elizabeth Devereaux.

(Above) Figure 48. Sandblasted clear tempered glass with sandblasted and gold-leafed interior panels by Sarah Hall for Michael Power Catholic School, Toronto, Canada.

(Right) Figure 49. Detail from "River of Light," an example of deeply "carved" sandblasted glass. Photos by André Beneteau.

Figure 50. The earliest painted image of Christ in stained glass to have survived intact (mid-eleventh century), located in the abbey church of Wissembourg, Alsace, France. Photo by Sarah Hall.

A Brief History of Stained Glass in Churches

Like a pebble tossed into a pond, the creation of a new stained glass window generates ripples that are felt long after the initial event. In commissioning a new work, a parish has the unique opportunity to make a meaningful contribution to the thousand-year history of this ancient and beautiful art. The history of stained glass is a fascinating one, and knowing it aids in the commissioning process.

Stained glass has been used in churches for over a millennium, and the windows created over the course of the centuries number in the hundreds of thousands. Many of these have been lost over time due to wars, fires, vandals, religious reformations and changing fashions. But enough windows remain to tell the fascinating tale of the development of this exceptional art form.

Early Uses

The earliest use of glass to ornament church windows dates well before written historical records. We do know that in the sixth century Saint Gregory had the windows of St. Martin Church in Tours, France, glazed with colored glass. However, it is fairly certain that early glasswork was undecorated and mounted in wood, stone or metal frames. Glasswork was mainly used to provide the church with light and protection from the elements, even after the introduction of images and decorations on glass.

Eventually, ideas and techniques from other art forms began to influence how glass was used in windows. Mosaics, cloisonne enamel and the jeweller's art of setting precious stones into gold and silver filigree all provided inspiration. Knights returning from the Crusades brought knowledge and admiration of Arabic windows, in which small pieces of colored glass were set into carved stucco or pierced marble fretwork. Illuminated manuscripts show a marked similarity in style and composition to the ornamental design of medieval windows.

However, two important technical discoveries were necessary for the development of stained glass as we know it. The first was the invention of milling, or casting, which produced the H-channel lead cames that hold the assembled pieces of glass together. The second was the development of glass paint, which allowed details such as facial features, hands and drapery to be painted onto glass. With these innovations, images began to be more commonly used in windows.

The earliest known stained glass images were based on Christian themes. These images were probably rather primitive in appearance, since glass offered a different surface to painters than plaster (frescoes) or wood panel (icons and altar screens). In time, however, technical advances, artistic innovation and a growing understanding of the unique qualities of glass brought medieval artists to a high level of artistry in the new medium.

The changing figure of Jesus Christ through various eras illustrates the development of stained glass in history. The Christian scriptures do not describe the physical appearance of Jesus. This posed little problem for the artists, however, since they were not trying to portray Jesus in a natural or historically accurate way. Instead, the purpose of medieval religious art was to create a visual symbol — an icon — that would draw viewers into the liturgy. In the windows of this period, the importance of the symbol overshadows everything else; every detail, each action and position reinforced

Figure 51. East window from

Poitiers cathedral (mid-eleventh

century) portraying a devotional

image of the crucifixion. Photo

by Peter Coffman.

the symbolic meaning of the figure. Despite the formality of this approach, artists of the time created distinctive and extraordinary works.

MEDIEVAL STAINED GLASS

Aside from fragments, the earliest existing painted image on stained glass is an image of the head of Christ. This extraordinary work, dating from around 1050, was excavated from the abbey church of Wissembourg, in Alsace, France (figure 51). It is now located in the Musée de l'Oeuvre Notre Dame in Strasbourg, France. The piece was created at a time when the fierce aesthetic of the Romanesque/Byzantine style reigned. Glass painters used simple, strong outlines, and backgrounds without depth or shading. These techniques endowed their work with immediacy and power. The austere, formal presentation and highly stylized linework portray Christ as solemn and magisterial — the "Conqueror Christ." The effectiveness of the work was strengthened by its setting, which was probably an unadorned leaded window of plain white glass. As the only painted element, the image would have appeared in this setting much as an icon.

Another outstanding image of Christ from the same period is found in the east window of Poitiers cathedral (figure 51). This remarkable window, dating from around 1160, shows Christ with deep blue hair and a body of pale violet on a bright red cross. Compared to the head of Christ from Wissembourg and other earlier windows, the window at Poitiers shows more animation and emotion. It also has a more ambitious iconography, containing the martyrdom of Saint Peter, the crucifixion and the resurrection, all in the same window. The highly stylized design and the colors embody the Romanesque approach characteristic of this period. The image of the open-eyed crucified Christ is given emphasis, towering over the other figures to its left and right. Although Christ is presented as crucified, he is not the man of sorrows — this Christ is without wounds or suffering.

With the advent of the Gothic style in the late twelfth and early thirteenth centuries, stained glass underwent a wondrous transformation. Structural innovations made it possible to provide much larger window openings, which were transformed into magnificent walls of color and light. Stained glass was no longer a decoration; it was an essential part of the fabric of the building.

More than an architectural or artistic trend, stained glass in this era was built on the theological groundwork laid by Abbot Suger at the Abbey of Saint Denis, north of Paris. Suger, inspired by the belief of the fifth-century writer Pseudo-Dionysius that visible things reveal the invisible, held that natural light mirrors the light of God. Suger filled his church with ornately jeweled objects and stained glass, the contemplation of which he regarded as a source of divine inspiration.

Figure 52. Grisaille windows at Yorkminster, known as the "Five Sisters" (mid-thirteenth century). Photo by Peter Coffman.

Even in medieval times, however, there was no universally accepted aesthetic for stained glass. While Abbot Suger was commissioning more and more gloriously colorful stained glass, an alternative movement was pushing for the elimination of color in church windows. The Cistercian order of monks, which preached the virtues of austerity and simplicity, issued a decree in 1134 proclaiming, "Let windows be of clear glass, without crosses or pictures." A further admonition came in 1182: "Stained glass windows are to be replaced within the space of two years; otherwise the abbot, prior and cellarer are henceforth all to fast on bread and water every sixth day until they are replaced." Perhaps the abbeys had been a little slow in destroying their colored stained glass windows!

Whether considerable stained glass was destroyed as a result of this iconoclastic Cistercian rule is unknown, but a window style called *grisaille* ("painted gray") evolved in response to this austere position. Leaded windows, based on foliage and geometric designs in clear and light tints, were made for the Cistercian abbeys (figures 52 and 53). Some grisaille windows were unpainted, while others were decorated with intricate and delicate paintwork. These light-filled windows possessed a quiet beauty that contrasted with the more colorful figurative and narrative windows. Most grisaille windows would not be out of place in a modern "minimalist" interior.

Figure 53. Detail from the "Five Sisters" showing its non-figurative, ornamental style of design. Photo by Sarah Hall.

The grisaille and colored styles have coexisted for centuries, but not always peaceably. There was, in fact, some conflict between the Cistercian champion Saint Bernard of Clairvaux and Abbot Suger, spurred by Bernard's criticisms of Suger's lavish abbey church, with its colorful and expensive windows. In response, Suger had his justification inscribed on the church doors of Saint Denis:

Figure 54. South transept rose window (mid-thirteenth century) from Chartres cathedral, based on images from the book of Revelation. Photo by William Lindsay.

> Whoever thou art, if thou seekest to extol the glory of these doors,
> marvel not at the gold and the expense but at the craftsmanship of the work.
> Bright is the noble work; but, being nobly bright, the work
> should brighten the minds, so that they may travel,
> through the true lights, to the True Light, where Christ is the true door.

Other substantial stained glass projects were executed during the Gothic period. Most of the glazing of Chartres cathedral took place during the thirteenth century, including the stunning south transept *rose window* (figure 54). The round, or "rose," window is a popular configuration for stained glass; the strength and spirituality projected by these circles of wondrous light is uniquely affecting. The south transept window at Chartres illustrates the vision that Saint John experienced on the island of Patmos toward the end of the first century, as described in the book of Revelation. The rose is made up of multi-form medallions depicting the four symbolic beasts of the Apocalypse, along with angels and elders who radiate outward from an image of Christ seated in judgement at the center of the rosette.

Realism in rose windows was considerably less important than structure and symbol. The arrangement of the spokes and other elements, which produces the Chartres window's exquisite flower-like effect, dominates the work. It is through this structure and the use of images that rose windows achieve the abstract qualities that make them seem to float in space.

Over the thirteenth and fourteenth centuries, significant changes took place in the portrayal of religious figures. The influence of the Franciscans, among others, helped shift religious art toward more realistic depictions of human beings. The humanization of Christ in art took place over decades, inspired by Giotto's precedent-setting frescoes in the upper church at Assisi, which depicted expressive faces of Jesus. This work clearly demonstrated a break with the formal, stylized Christ of Romanesque/Byzantine art. Under these influences, and through a steady process of artistic and technical development, Christ as portrayed in stained glass gradually became less distant and severe, becoming tender, gentle and heroic.

Figure 55. Detail of "Pieta" (mid-fifteenth century) from the east window of Holy Trinity Church, Long Melford, Suffolk, England. Photo by Sarah Hall.

Technical and architectural advances in the fourteenth century also effected the production of stained glass. The discovery of silver stain ushered in new artistic styles, while improved glassmaking techniques made possible the production of larger pieces of glass, which in turn led to an increased ability to naturalize human figures. In addition to becoming more humanized, depictions of Christ were able to shed the mosaic appearance that characterized earlier images of him in church windows.

By the fifteenth century, Christ was most often portrayed as the Son of Man, completing his transformation from a hieratic symbol to a human figure. This development led to many portrayals of the suffering Christ, and Christ's passion was a prevalent subject (figure 55).

RENAISSANCE STAINED GLASS

The image of Christ continued to evolve during the Renaissance. The increasingly sophisticated use of paint and silver stain facilitated his continued humanization in stained glass and allowed powerful portrayals of emotion and suffering. As the period progressed, images of Christ's suffering gave way to an emphasis on his perfect humanity.

A second trend toward increasingly accurate anatomy, perspective and realism posed more problems for stained glass artists, who found themselves at a disadvantage in comparison to canvas painters. Realistic figures looked out of place and unconvincing when surrounded by heavy lines of lead. In response, artists used larger pieces of glass and glass paints to try to achieve a three-dimensional modeled effect (figure 56). This indeed brought increased realism, but it also weakened the connection between figure and material; the glass became little more than a canvas for what was, in essence, a painting. With the growing disconnection between the image, the shape of the glass and its architectural setting, the fundamental character of stained glass as an art form was lost.

Increasing realism also made stained glass less suitable as an architectural art. In a large church, a clerestory window may be as much as 100 feet from the eyes of the viewer. While simpler and more iconographic figures could be recognized from that distance, the subtlety of the more realistic figures, with real-life features and emotions, was easily missed by the viewer.

The Protestant Reformation brought further changes to stained glass. Hundreds of windows were destroyed for their perceived idolatry, and the new windows in Protestant churches favored heraldry and historical themes over religious imagery.

The introduction of enamel paints, which allowed artists to use many colors on a single sheet of glass, was the beginning of the end for the traditional art of stained glass. With this technique, glazing became secondary to painting, as sheets of white glass were cut to larger, more regular patterns and painted in full-color enamel. Leads no longer played any part in the design: The pieces of enameled glass were held in a geometric, metal armature (figure 57). Although this medium was popular for a time, glass painted in this way possessed none of the brilliance and transparency of colored, handblown glass. In addition, enameled glass was less durable; over time the enamels flaked and peeled off, leaving fragmented, unattractive images that are today almost impossible to restore.

Figure 56. "Betrayal" (mid-sixteenth century) from St. Mary's Church, Shrewsbury, shows the increased realism and perspective attempted in stained glass windows during the Renaissance. Photo by Sarah Hall.

(Above) Figure 57. Affectionately

known as one of the "Washy

Virtues," this detail is from Joshua

Reynolds's enamel painted windows

(mid-eighteenth century) at New

College Chapel, Oxford, England,

and clearly shows the radical

change from the leaded windows of

colored glass of the medieval

period. Photo by Sarah Hall.

(Right) Figure 58. Interior of

St. Martin-in-the-Fields,

London (1721 – 26),

by architect James Gibbes.

Photo by Peter Coffman.

AN ALMOST LOST ART

Although these enameled windows were made of glass, they were no longer "stained glass" as we know it. True stained glass was on its way to becoming a lost art. The development of the Baroque and Rococo styles of architecture threatened even these poor windows. The gilded interiors and painted ceilings of Baroque churches needed abundant clear light to be seen. Traditional stained glass was considered heavy, dark and primitive-looking. Colored light in a church emphasized mystery, but religious focus in the period had moved toward preaching and scripture. The "Age of Enlightenment" desired a clear, lucid light to illuminate the church and make visible the rationality of its classically detailed geometric interiors (figure 58).

The misfortunes of stained glass during this period are well summarized by George Seddon: "The medieval art of stained glass was the offspring of the Catholic Church. It was born in northern Europe in the eleventh century, spent a magnificent youth there during the great Cathedral Age, traveled widely in southern Europe as it matured, and died in the sixteenth century, slowly poisoned by the Renaissance and, finally, stabbed in the back by the Reformation" (Lawrence Lee, George Seddon and Francis Stephens, *Stained Glass* [London: Michael Beazley Publishers, Ltd., 1976], page 124).

For nearly two centuries stained glass was in decline. The methods for making colored glass were neglected and the techniques of traditional glass painting and silver staining rarely practiced. However, the revival of interest in all

Figure 59. Interior of All Saints Church, Margaret Street, London (1850–59), by architect William Butterfield, showing Gothic Revival style architecture. Photo by Peter Coffman.

things medieval and the building of neo-Gothic churches in the nineteenth century (figure 59) spurred an effort to recreate the art of stained glass. Renowned Gothic Revivalist Augustus Pugin (the younger of the two Augustus Pugins) himself designed stained glass windows (figure 60).

REVIVAL AND MASS PRODUCTION

The obsession in nineteenth-century Europe with Gothic architecture, medieval legends and arts was widespread, but it was not always accompanied by a deep understanding of what was being emulated. External medieval forms could be imitated, but it was impossible to recapture the spirit of the age that created those forms. Nevertheless, the Gothic Revivalists put a great deal of energy into reconstructing, understanding and preserving medieval stained glass. They managed to rediscover and recreate many of the techniques of medieval window builders.

But there were other influences at work. Pietism, along with the social and artistic cultures of the time, began to steer religious art toward sentimentality. The image of Jesus in the nineteenth century became the gentle Savior, with soft features and a sad expression. Unfortunately for stained glass, this stylistic cul-de-sac was reached just as a boom in church building brought mass production to what had once been an architecturally responsive and unique art form.

Due to the endless reuse of Victorian-era designs and images, what may have otherwise been a passing stylistic phase became ingrained in the public mind as "real" stained glass. These designs were pressed into service hundreds of times with little or no regard for the architectural setting. The popular Victorian image of Christ as the "Light of the World" exemplifies this trend. Hundreds of stained glass studios made copies of this famous painting by Holman Hunt, continuously reproducing it well into the twentieth century, which resulted in thousands upon thousands of uninspired, lifeless copies littering modern churches

Figure 60. Gothic Revival style window by Augustus Pugin for Sts. Mary and David Church, Kilpeck, Herefordshire, England. Photo by Peter Coffman.

(figure 61). Stained glass was thus reduced to a "religious art product," rather than a practiced art and craft that allowed room for inspiration and originality.

THE ARTS AND CRAFTS MOVEMENT

Fortunately, copies of Gothic windows, Victorian sentimentality and mass production were not universally embraced in the nineteenth century. One influential dissenter was the British designer William Morris. In 1842, at eight years of age, William was taken by his father to Canterbury Cathedral. It was, he recalled as if the gates of heaven had been opened to him. Morris and his compatriots believed artists should be inspired by the best of medieval arts and crafts. While he acknowledged the "outburst of genius" that took place in the Renaissance, he did not agree with its precise and academic artistic style. Morris was not a Gothic Revivalist but rather an innovator with a deep respect for medievalism and for the satisfaction that skilled craftsmanship can afford the practitioner.

Morris and his compatriots introduced naturalism and beautiful figures into the many media in which they worked. In stained glass, the windows of the Arts and Crafts movement avoided the overly pious sentimentality that characterized Victorian work and reestablished lead-lines as an elegant and vital part of the design. It is from this artistic thread that much of modern stained glass is woven.

An early outgrowth of the Arts and Crafts movement in America was the stained glass of Louis Comfort Tiffany. A technical innovator in glass manufacture as well as a talented designer and landscape painter, Tiffany was inspired by the natural world. His use of textured and iridescent glass was well suited to the romantic, pastoral landscapes he designed, and his designs worked well as domestic windows. When he entered the world of ecclesiastical art, he found himself embroiled in controversies over both his approach to subject matter and the type of glass he used.

Tiffany's one-time friend — and then rival — John La Farge was successful in both figurative and landscape drawing, which gave him an edge in ecclesiastical commissions. Although Tiffany's studio designers did their share of figurative windows, Tiffany himself did not possess strong skills in this area. Moreover, he faced resistance to his pastoral landscapes being accepted as church windows. He hoped his windows would find a religious resonance with American congregations, and indeed the "iconoclastic" churches such as the Baptists, Unitarians and Congregationalists welcomed his landscape designs. In designing windows for churches, he carefully selected symbolic flowers and vines, combining them with light-filled allegorical scenery.

The prevailing church architecture in America at the turn of the twentieth century, however, was still Gothic Revival, and these churches were designed to have Gothic Revival windows, that is, work made with transparent, handmade glass, painted and leaded in mosaic-style windows. In 1905, when one of Tiffany's largest pictorial windows was commissioned for a church designed by Ralph Adams Cram, an eminent architect of the Gothic Revival, a bitter war of words erupted. Tiffany's design, made in *opalescent* glass, featured a sensuous romantic landscape glimpsed through the branches of an enormous tree. It showed a complete disregard for the architectural setting and window *tracery*.

Figure 61. Holman Hunt's Victorian painting, "Light of the World," by Robert McCausland Studios, Toronto, Canada. Photo by Sarah Hall.

Figure 62. "Le Christ aux outrages"
(1939) by Georges Roualt, exhibited
at the Petit-Palais exhibition in
Paris and later installed in
Notre-Dame-de-Toute-Grace
at Assy. Photo by Sarah Hall.

This pictorial approach had more in common with enamel painting and the "illuminated canvases" of the seventeenth and eighteenth centuries. It resulted in a barrage of criticism, particularly from the architect, who loathed the window and considered it irreligious. It was, however, a popular success.

Tiffany's turn-of-the-century artwork has evoked both contempt and adulation over the years, but there is no doubt that he was a remarkable maker of opulent landscapes. Whether they transcend their dreamy, romantic quality to communicate a spiritual message is still a question.

As the Arts and Crafts movement rediscovered the potential of stained glass, its enthusiasm sometimes overshadowed good aesthetic judgement. The hodge-podge of window "styles," some pictorial art glass, others Gothic Revival, that are often found in churches of this era is generally a reflection of various donors' tastes. This mix gives these churches the curious air of a museum rather than the dignity of a place for liturgy.

MIDDLE AND LATE TWENTIETH CENTURY

Art in the twentieth century has been shaped by many factors — artistic, historical and social. Developments in painting and sculpture, including the different movements in abstract art, have had a profound effect on stained glass. The failed attempts at realism in Renaissance and Victorian styles alike have inspired caution in glass artists, especially when using figures. Some avoid figures altogether; others use figures but create them in a highly personal style. The images of Christ found in these modern styles reflect many different approaches, which often reveal as much about the artist as they do about the subject.

Many of the twentieth century images of Christ portray him as the man of sorrows, presenting an image of Christ the Redeemer. On the eve of World War II, French painter George Roualt created his own image of the sorrowful Christ, "Le Christ aux outrages," for an exhibition at the Petit-Palais in Paris. The window was later installed by Father Marie-Alain Couturier, along with other windows Roualt had designed, at Notre-Dame-de-Toute-Grace at Plateau d'Assy (figure 62). Although his windows caused an uproar, they are today among the most famous stained glass windows in France.

As Abbot Suger was in his time, Father Marie-Alain Couturier, a French Dominican priest and leading light of the Sacred Art movement of the 1930s, was vitally influential in the modern development of stained glass. All great art, he believed, was holy, connected to the creativity of God. This belief, and more importantly his active involvement in commissioning new work, set the theological stage for contemporary art, which was increasingly abstract and personal, to find a place in churches.

Figure 63. Resurrection window

(1964) by Georg Meistermann

in the Catholic parish church

in Bad Kissingen, Germany.

Photo by Sarah Hall.

Couturier was determined to bring ecclesiastical art out of the ghetto of provincialism and kitsch. His writings in the publication *Art Sacre,* which he began editing in 1937, fueled public disagreements between the supporters of figurative stained glass and those of abstract. Exceptional contributions to the art of stained glass came from the leading artists in France — Leger, Mattise, Braque, Manessier, Villon and Chagall. This collaboration between artists and the church was a turning point for stained glass in the twentieth century and a springboard for the full flowering of a modern style that was soon to take place in Germany.

The terrible wars of the first part of the century had a significant effect on art and the church. In addition to the human tragedies wrought by World Wars I and II, many thousands of churches and cathedrals were destroyed. The wars had a profound social impact as well, clearing away old social structures and certainties, and infusing subsequent generations with a distrust of the old and a hunger for the new.

Postwar Germany was especially affected by this change; within a generation its stained glass artists completely rejected a tradition of sentimental and idealized painted images and embraced a dramatic and uncompromising return to the eloquence of unpainted glass and strong linework. The extensive rebuilding program of churches in Germany, many with vast walls of stained glass, was met by this exceptional generation of designers. The unspoken guideline dictated that new buildings must be constructed with new materials and new concepts. Remarkably, the number of new churches built in Germany in the 20 years between 1950 and 1970 was greater than the number built in the 400 years between 1545 and 1945!

Georg Meistermann, professor of fine art at the Dusseldorf Academy, was among the first and foremost postwar German artists to design stained glass. In Germany the stained glass "studio system" separated artists and craftsman so that most designs were carried out by freelance artists rather than in-house artist-designers. Meistermann, however, was a skilled draftsman with a profound religious imagination. His dynamic compositions hover between abstraction and expressionism, often using the most elemental of stained glass techniques: handmade leaded glass and perhaps a little paint. In his "Resurrection" window (figure 63), the figure of Christ, while clearly present, is so fully integrated into the composition that there is no differentiation made between background, foreground and figure, or between the figure and the subject of the window itself.

In a work by Kenneth von Roenn, Jr., for Christ Church Cathedral in Louisville, Kentucky, the figure of Christ is presented as a symbol of universal dualities. Two figures have been superimposed: a male figure from Gothic sculpture and a female dancer. The male figure, painted in black, is visible during the day from the interior of the church. In the evening the female dancer, painted in white, is visible from the exterior. This multi-faceted image of light and dark, male and female, stone and flesh, static and fluid, finds echoes in contemporary theology.

In an age of expanding horizons and new techniques, artistic visions have moved contemporary stained glass into a realm of layered images and meaning. This is to be expected, since the realism of the Victorians was made superfluous by the realism of the photograph, computer image and high-definition television. Current artwork is often a reflection, meditation or interpretation of Christian concerns, resulting in deeply-felt religious works that evoke the presence of Christ for the Christian viewer.

In his controversial "Physics" window (figure 64) for Holy Ghost Church in Heidelberg, Germany, artist Johannes Schrieter juxtaposes biblical text with an image of an atom bomb and the date of the bombing of Hiroshima, August 8, 1945. The first biblical text is from Peter 3:10: "But the day of the Lord will come as a thief, and then the heavens will pass away with a loud noise, and the elements will be dissolved with fire, and the earth and everything that is done on it will be disclosed" (NRSV). The second text, Isaiah 54:10, reads: "For the mountains may depart, and the hills be removed, but my steadfast love shall not depart from you, and my covenant of peace shall not be removed, says the Lord, who has compassion on you" (NRSV).

In past ages, artists, architects, clergy and congregations have built their churches and created stained glass to express their own times. Contemporary glasswork has developed organically out of the forms that preceded it, yet it still lies within a continuum. In creating stained glass for places for liturgy today, those commissioning stained glass must question the notion that imitating the style of a past age or simply using biblical scenes makes an artwork "religious." It seems that this notion of the meaning of "religious" veers too close to sentimentality. Great church architecture and great stained glass are always genuine expressions in, of and for their own time.

(Opposite page) Figure 64. "Physics" window by Johannes Schrieter (1984) for Holy Ghost Church, Heidelberg, Germany, in which biblical texts are juxtaposed with an image of an atom bomb and the date of the bombing of Hiroshima. Photo by Sarah Hall.

Figure 65.

"Holy Spirit"

window by Jim

Piercey, Canterbury

Episcopal Retreat, Oviedo,

Florida (1995). Photo by Jim Piercey.

DESIGN

A good design gives structure, beauty and meaning to a stained glass window. The window design has to work within the total environment of the building, taking into account the building's architecture, the quality of light, and the needs and expectations of the building's users.

When the window is in a church, there is another factor: the window's spiritual role in the environment for liturgy. Stained glass has the unique ability to modify the visual environment by adding color and form to the space, thereby changing the nature of light itself. In a church, this visual experience can serve as a bridge to the spiritual. Achieving this is not always easy, as such work requires a high level of care and commitment from both the artist and the church community. But what is the point of making church windows that do not connect to something beyond themselves?

Much of the commissioning process is concerned with design, and the text below offers an overview of the design process, as well as the terminology used in describing window designs. Details of the commissioning process are covered in the next chapter.

In a commissioned window, the design is developed and proposed by a stained glass artist or studio and reviewed by the client. Once the client approves the design, fabrication of the window begins. In the case of a church commission, the whole parish is the client, and it is usually represented by a committee. Sometimes a person of authority within the church, such as the pastor, takes charge, but more often the building, renovation or art committee represents the parish.

As the group that manages the commissioning process and gives final approval to the design, the committee has the important responsibility of getting the best possible design for the window. It can do this in three ways: through its choice of the artist or studio; through the information and guidance it gives the artist or studio at the beginning of the design process; and through its interaction with the artist or studio during the completion of the final design.

THE DESIGNER

When choosing a designer, the committee should start by researching what artists and studios are available. For a small window, the committee will probably want to limit its search to local artists, provided there are enough to choose from. For larger windows or a series of windows, however, the committee should broaden its search so that it is able to review a full range of possible artists.

It may also be helpful for committee members to view a variety of windows at other churches at this time and then discuss what works and doesn't work in each. As they do so, members should keep in mind that they are not "shopping" for a window but rather increasing their understanding and appreciation of windows in general. This will improve their ability to commission and critique a window design for their own church.

The selection process itself may take several forms, depending on the range of studios being considered, the size of the commission, the available budget and the level of artistic knowledge among the committee members. Sometimes a decision is made on the basis of the previous work of artists and studios; in other cases, a design competition is held. The next chapter will discuss these options in more detail.

Figure 66. Chapel windows for

Fortbildungsstatte des Erzbistums,

Hamburg, Germany,

by Johannes Beeck (1996).

Fabricated by Derix Studios.

Photo by Wilhelm Derix.

If the committee is looking for an original work and has arranged for presentations of previous works by artists and studios, the members should remember that the windows presented to them were designed for specific locations and situations. A design commissioned by the committee may not look like any of those presented. Rather than focus on individual windows, the members should try to decide which of the presenters has produced work that is generally most appropriate to its own church. In addition, the committee's decision should be based on whether members feel they can work with the artist (who is either independent or an in-house designer in a firm) in the process of developing and approving a window design.

In choosing an artist or studio, the committee will probably be dealing with one or both of two main types of stained glass studio: a commercial studio that both designs and fabricates the windows; or an independent artist's studio that either fabricates the windows in-house or contracts with another studio to assist with the fabrication. Each takes a different approach to designing stained glass, and it is up to the committee to make sure that the approach used is the one it wants for the church's windows. A little background information can help the members ask the right questions.

Commercial Studios

There are two main types of commercial studios: those that offer original designs and those that copy extant ones. Most commercial studios have an in-house designer; if this person is doing original work, the designs can be quite worthwhile, provided the designer is given enough time and support for this part of the work. Sometimes these designers will only produce work in a particular "studio style," and the committee will need to consider this type of work on its own merits.

In some studios, the in-house "designer" is really a "recycler" who adapts old designs to the size and shape of the window ordered. The reasons for this are primarily economic.

Despite its essential importance to the quality of a stained glass window, design is the element that most often gets shortchanged. Although this can happen no matter who designs the window, in some commercial studios such shortcuts are standard policy. These studios, many of which have been in business for decades, have accumulated a large number of designs from previous projects and have kept all of their cartoons (full-size drawings). Additionally, they may have purchased cartoons from other studios that have closed. With this collection of designs, these studios can endlessly reproduce older windows with only minor changes to accommodate variations in window size and shape.

Figure 67. Chapel windows for

St. Nikolaus, Braunschweig,

Germany, by Gunter Grohs (1995).

Fabricated by Derix Studios.

Photo by Wilhelm Derix.

Figure 68. Gethsemani window,

Munich, Germany, by

Jürgen Reipka (1998).

Fabricated by Sattler Studio.

Photo by Norbert Sattler.

The economic advantages of such an approach are obvious: Creating a full-size working drawing for a figurative window—especially a large window with several figures—requires tremendous time, talent and expense. Clients given a choice between original work at one price and copied windows at a slightly lower price will generally choose the latter, especially if they don't understand (or don't care about) the difference. This approach offers the studio practical advantages as well. Not only is time saved by reusing old work, the ordering process is relatively risk-free. All the studio has to do is gather up a catalog of its standard

designs, and clients can then pick and choose their windows, just as they do their pews and offering baskets.

Although the business advantages to this approach are clear, the windows that result tend to be an artistically sorry lot. Usually based on Victorian-era paintings, these windows are marked by sentimentality, an over-painted heaviness and a formulaic portrayal of biblical scenes. Moreover, the designs are often simply laid over whatever window shape is needed, such that any relationship between the window and the building's architecture is purely coincidental.

Figure 69. The windows in Rogate Church, Hamburg-Meiendorf, Germany, by Beate Wassermann (1995). Fabricated by Derix Studios. Photo by Wilhelm Derix.

Independent Artist's Studios

Although an independent artist's studio can also provide both design and fabrication services, it differs from a commercial studio in that the artist is a designer first and foremost. An independent artist's reputation depends on the quality of her or his designs. For this reason, an independent artist's studio offers strong advantages. There is a dedication to service and an understanding of the importance of design that is rare in larger operations. Sometimes the individual artist subcontracts the fabrication of the windows to another studio, but she or he nonetheless supervises the fabrication and takes responsibility for it.

Choosing a Studio

Whatever type of stained glass studio the committee chooses, be it a commercial studio, an independent artist's studio or a studio solely for fabrication, the important thing to remember is that it is primarily the design that will determine whether the window is successful or not. No studio, whatever its size, reputation or number of years in business, can make a good window from a bad design.

Figure 70. Window in St. Basil Church, Toronto, Canada, by N. T. Lyons (1913). Photo by Sarah Hall.

STYLE

Once the committee has selected an artist or designer, it will work with him or her to develop a common understanding of what is desired in the windows. This includes concept, style, preferred colors, and so on. In this process, good communication is essential and requires a common understanding of terms and ideas. Some of the elements will depend on other plans that are being made or have been realized in the building — the interior color scheme, for example. But one of the first elements that needs to be discussed is style.

"Style" is shorthand used to describe a particular artistic approach to design. Stained glass done in a certain style will use color, line, figures and shapes in a way that recognizably belongs to a particular era or artistic movement. Style, while a convenient way to categorize windows, is a very rough guide to a window's artistic content, and not every window can be categorized in this way. Nevertheless, it is useful to understand what types of windows fit within the commonly referenced styles. The following is a survey of some of the styles of windows being made today.

Traditional

This is a commonly used term with an extraordinarily vague meaning. With a thousand years of stained glass to turn to, the question inevitably arises, "Which tradition?" In Europe this may well mean medieval windows. In North America, with our much shorter history, "traditional" often refers to Victorian or Gothic Revival style windows.

Windows in the Victorian traditional style are characterized by the use of colored, transparent glass that is fairly heavily painted to achieve perspective and portray accurate details. They may have a single figure with a background, or they may contain more narrative scenes with groups of figures. These windows attempt to re-create in leaded glass the look of eighteenth-century enamel painting and possess a pervasive sentimentality throughout (figure 70).

The other major stained glass tradition in North America, Gothic Revival, produced windows with a different look and more strength of character than their Victorian cousins. Based on the richly colored, mosaic appearance of medieval windows, these narrative-based windows found homes in many Gothic Revival churches in the United States and Canada (figure 71).

Tiffany or Art Glass

Tiffany glass, also known as art glass, refers to windows either designed by Louis Comfort Tiffany himself or to windows designed in a similar style that use the opalescent glass he is famous for developing. This style is closely related to the Art Nouveau movement, which flourished around the beginning of the twentieth century, and to the American School of landscape painting.

In Tiffany windows there is usually very little painting done on the glass; the lead-lines themselves provide the "drawing." Heavy textures and ripples in the glass itself sometimes provide dimensional characteristics. The overall effect of the window is translucent rather than transparent, and sensuous rather than austere. Windows are still being created in this style, sometimes as Tiffany copies and sometimes

(Above) Figure 71. Window in St. Jude Church, Oakville, Ontario, Canada, by Yvonne Williams (1949). Photo by William Lindsay.

(Left) Figure 72. Window held by the Morse Collection, Winter Park, Orlando, Florida, by Louis Comfort Tiffany (1903). Photo by Sarah Hall.

with new designs, although these are more often created for domestic settings rather than for churches (figure 72).

Modern

This term is as vague as "traditional," if not more so. Within the definition of "modern" are a number of other imprecise terms — "abstract," "symbolic" and "contemporary" — which seem to be used interchangeably. This terminology is confusing and arbitrary, and can lead to difficulties in expressing the actual appearance of a window.

Some modern windows are figurative or semi-figurative. In modern windows, the artist generally gives the figure and the theme it represents a personal interpretation and drawing style. The figures may be hand-painted or created

Figure 73. Screen-painted Pentecost panel from St. Andrew Catholic Church, Columbus, Ohio, by Sarah Hall (1997). Photo by Peter Coffman. (Facing page) Figure 74. "New Jerusalem" window, Christ the King Church, Dunbar, West Virginia, by David Wilson (1983). Photo by David Wilson.

through the use of screened images (figure 73). In figurative work, individual glass pieces are given a number of treatments, which may include painting, silver staining and etching in various combinations. Some figurative windows are unpainted and rely on leadwork to achieve the effect of drawing. Other windows use minimal paint along with a strong graphic approach. The ability to create engaging figurative windows without the use of paint takes exceptional drafts-manship and imagination. When it succeeds, the results can be extraordinary.

Some modern windows are "narrative" in that the artist is interpreting a specific theme or religious concept. This can take the form of a literal depiction, or it may be expressed with a more abstract, stylized approach. In designing this type of window, some artists will rely on well-known Christian symbols, while others may work within the context of a more personal and idiosyncratic artistic language. Both of these approaches can find happy homes in today's churches

and offer a deeply considered reflection of the commissioning congregation.

Modern buildings generally require modern stained glass due to the compatibility of materials, texture and transparency, as well as to similar values in line and color. The integration between the window as an architectural element and the building it serves is crucial. Examples of both modern and historic buildings in which the architecture and the stained glass are badly matched are all too common.

This lack of integration can also occur when parishes are tempted to rescue old windows from closed church buildings and recycle them in newer ones. While it is good to preserve good quality stained glass and better to install it in a church than in a restaurant, it is an exceedingly difficult task requiring great skill. It almost requires designing the building to fit the preexistent windows. It is simply impossible to successfully take a window that was originally placed in a Gothic Revival window opening in a wall of limestone block that is 50 feet tall, leave out the pointed arch segments, and cram it into a rectangular window opening in a modern brick wall that is only 30 feet tall. Such an installation does not do justice to the window or the wall, and the result will be unsatisfactory from an artistic and historical perspective.

Contemporary Pattern-based or Ornamental
Ornamental windows — those strictly decorative and unpainted — were the first to be used in churches, and this was the predominant form of glazing for centuries. Even before the use of glass in windows, iron or wood frames were used to hold pieces of thinly sliced alabaster, horn or bone in window openings, allowing light into the space while protecting the interior from the elements. The wood or iron lattice became more elaborate over time, and glass was introduced as the most precious and expensive glazing available.

Although most people are more familiar with the richly figurative and narrative Gothic windows, there has also been a parallel tradition of decorative and ornamental glass through the centuries, such as the grisaille style, which used little or no color. Versions of this style are still being used today.

(Opposite page) Figure 75. Georg Meistermann has created an expressive interpretation of "Jesus Walking on Water," St. Mary Church, Koln Kalk, Germany, (1964). Photo by Sarah Hall.

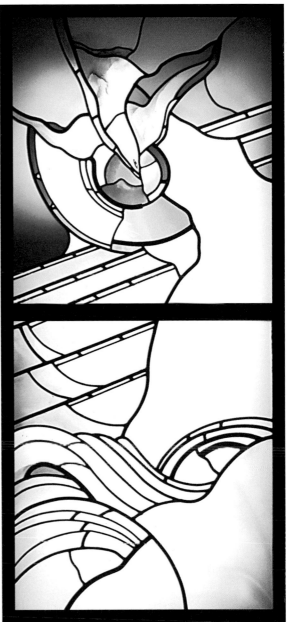

(Above) Figure 76. This window detail from Pentz United Church, Nova Scotia, Canada, by Anita Rist-Geiger is based on the Holy Spirit and the element of air (1996). Photo by Sarah Hall.

(Left) Figure 77. A window based on the themes of "Faith, Hope and Charity" by Georg Meistermann (1962). Photo by Sarah Hall.

(Opposite page) Figure 78. Kenneth von Roenn, Jr., expressed the significance of water as a symbol of spiritual regeneration in this window for the Carmelite Monastery in Indianapolis, Indiana (1988). Photo by Kenneth von Roenn, Jr.

(Left) Figure 79. Paul's journey and revelation are the themes expressed in the "Road to Damascus" window for St. Paul the Apostle Catholic Church in Burlington, Ontario, Canada, by Sarah Hall (1989). Photo by William Lindsay.

Contemporary windows based on patterns or ornamentation are often a good fit with modern buildings. Their ability to modulate light, echo the lines and structure of the building, and release the viewer from an overly didactic environment can be a refreshing and welcome addition to a church.

DESIGN, FINALIZATION AND APPROVAL

Once the design process begins, the committee must strike a delicate balance between overseeing the design and trusting the artist enough to let the design develop. This is a dynamic process in which the committee learns about the artist (and stained glass) even as the artist is learning about the particular church building and its congregation. Both artist and committee are taking some risks in this process, and the chance for success will be greatest if there is mutual trust and respect.

In designing a window, an artist draws fully on all of his or her resources; training, experience and artistry are combined with a deepening understanding

Figure 80. Kenneth von Roenn, Jr.,

created windows with a

Cistercian-like quality in this

restoration of the sanctuary

for Battell Chapel at

Yale University (1987).

Photo by Kenneth von Roenn, Jr.

Figure 81. David Wilson's

"Communion of Saints" window

at St. Paul, Tampa, Florida

(1990). Photo by David Wilson.

of the spiritual, architectural and social context into which the window will be placed. In order to integrate these disparate elements and create an artwork of beauty, structure and meaning, the artist must rely on that most important of elements, inspiration. Inspiration is a powerful creative force, but it is not a straightforward or predictable one. As the artist works, the drawings begin to take on a life of their own. It is out of this act of creativity, faith and inspiration that the design takes shape.

In reviewing the artist's proposal for the window or windows, the committee may find that the design isn't exactly what was expected. It is worth remembering that today's familiar styles of stained glass are the culmination of thousands of innovations over the art form's long history. Every one of these innovations came about because somebody had the courage to challenge the accepted notions of what religious art should look like.

Within any given century there is some work that is artistically and technically adventurous, and other work that reflects advances in theological concepts. While it is not absolutely necessary for a commissioning committee to be on the cutting edge, it is essential that it be open-minded about what might be best for its church.

(Left and right) Figures 82 and 83. Anita Rist-Geiger's windows based on Saint Afra and Saint Ulrich for Hochaltingen Catholic Church, Germany (1990). Photo by Norbert Sattler.

Figure 84. Jim Piercey's abstract

"Eucharist" window provides

a beautiful prismatic and

sculptural field behind the

tabernacle at St. Peter the

Apostle Catholic Church,

Naples, Florida (1995).

Photo by Jim Piercey.

Figure 85. David Wilson's abstract window wall, "The Field Is White and Ready to Harvest," Reorganized Church of Jesus Christ of Latter Day Saints, Independence, Missouri (1992). Photo by David Wilson.

Commissioning Stained Glass

Every church window is a team effort. Committee members and clergy, members of the congregation, donors, architects, builders, stained glass artists and craftspeople all have a hand in the process. The artistic and technical quality of the final product will depend a lot on how well this team works together. This puts great responsibility on the committee managing the project, but it can be done well. By being informed and organized, by understanding the challenges, managing the connections, and making good decisions based on sound information, the committee will be able to complete the process successfully, from initial meetings through final installation.

As a stained glass window is planned, designed and built, the role of the committee managing the process goes through four main phases: planning for the windows, choosing an artist, design and fabrication, and installation and celebration. An overview of the phases is provided below, followed by a more detailed explanation of each phase.

Planning for the Windows

The planning phase is the time for committee members to be gathering information, getting organized, and establishing timelines and milestones for the commissioning process. The committee can begin to discuss what kind of window is desired, the budget and resources that are available, and any limitations that may apply. It can also begin to plan the overall process that will be followed, including what method will be used to identify and evaluate artists in the selection phase. By the end of the phase, work responsibilities should be clear, and a budget and preliminary schedule

established. The committee can then begin the process of selecting an artist or studio.

Choosing an Artist

The process of choosing an artist can go in different directions, depending on the plans made in the first phase. The committee may schedule a series of studio presentations, or it may hold an open competition. A competition begins with an invitation to stained glass artists to send slides of previous work. The committee then narrows the field to between two and five artists, who are then paid to produce designs for the windows. The committee then selects from among the submitted designs.

Whatever the selection method used, the committee's responsibility is to be well organized and to manage the process efficiently and fairly. At the end of this part of the process, the committee must choose an artist or studio to work with. It can then begin to make arrangements with the artist for finalization of the design, contracts and schedules. The members will also want to let the wider community know of the committee's decision. (All references to "the artist" in this chapter are meant to apply to anyone doing original designs — whether she or he is working independently or as an in-house designer for a studio.)

Design and Fabrication

In the design and fabrication phase, the committee works with the selected artist, completing the task of reviewing and approving the final design, and begins to shift its energy to managing the rest of the process. If it has not already done so, the committee will need to raise funds to pay for the construction and installation of the windows. Some projects begin with the money in hand. Others find it more helpful to have the final designs available to show people when soliciting funds. This second approach may mean that there is a significant lag between the completion of the design and its fabrication.

The rest of the committee's task is to monitor the building of the window, keeping track of the costs and making sure that schedules are being followed.

INSTALLATION AND CELEBRATION

In this fourth phase, the contractor, site supervisor and artist set schedules for delivery, scaffold arrangements and installation of the work. The committee can then begin planning for the dedication ceremonies.

THE COMMISSIONING PROCESS STEP BY STEP

The following outline is a guide to commissioning stained glass based on the four phases described above. For each of the phases, there are answers to some commonly asked questions. Additionally, three of the phases have "to do" lists to help the committee get started in its work.

Planning for the Windows

"To Do" List

1. Form a committee or designate a person who has the authority to act for the church. (Throughout the rest of this chapter, "committee" will be used to denote whoever is managing the process, recognizing that this may be referring to a single person.)

2. Determine the decision-making process of the committee: For example, will the committee make decisions based on majority rule or rule by consensus? ("Rule by consensus" indicates that the committee discusses an issue until a decision is reached that everyone can live with. It may not be everyone's first choice, but all agree to trust the decision.)

3. Select a spokesperson or chairperson.

4. Prepare a brief statement concerning the windows: Why does the parish want these stained glass windows? What is the purpose of the windows? What will they mean to the parish?

5. Identify all of the windows, interior glass screens and entryways that will be considered for art glass, and note their dimensions and square footage. The building's architect can supply this information.

6. Set schedules and budget parameters.

7. Establish how the committee's information and decisions will be communicated to the wider community: Bulletin or newsletter articles, announcements at liturgy, and town-hall meetings are all possible choices.

8. Determine the relationship of donors to the decision-making process and how their contributions will be acknowledged.

9. Research the available artists or studios. Create a list of artists to be contacted.

10. Visit other churches to see and compare artists' work. In light of these visits, discuss what members want or don't want in the parish's stained glass windows.

11. Determine the method of artist selection — interviews, holding a competition, and so on.

12. Send a request to artists for their *curricula vitae,* slides, brochures, videos and references based on previous work; include information about your project from numbers 4 and 5 above.

13. Review artists' materials; create a short list of between two and five artists.

14. Prepare a letter to the chosen artists, inviting them to present their previous work or to participate in a competition.

15. Choose an artist based on the selection method being used.

QUESTIONS AND ANSWERS

Who should be on the committee?

The committee should be large enough to have a good range of interests without being unwieldy; five to ten people is a good size. It is a good idea to involve the architect (for a new building or addition), clergy or staff with some knowledge about art and design, and representatives of the congregation. The committee should also include someone with the authority to make decisions for the church.

While people with previous experience in commissioning art are a useful addition to the committee, it is safe to say that most volunteers will be new to it. A willingness to donate time and effort, and to learn about stained glass, is almost as valuable as experience — sometimes more so. Potential volunteers may be hesitant to get involved with what they fear could be a complicated and time-consuming project. At the same time, many volunteers care deeply about what happens to their building and want to have a say in the works of art that go into it. If those initiating the project are clear about the time and work commitment, they can help allay any fears.

There will probably be one or two members who have strong personal opinions about art, and their likes and dislikes can have an overwhelming influence on the rest of the committee. It is important for everyone on the committee to look beyond their own personal tastes to see what will best suit the building and the intended use of the space. A balance of viewpoints among the membership and a diplomatic chairperson can help keep the committee on track.

Are there alternatives to committees?

The church can ask a liturgical consultant, an art consultant or its architectural firm to research, screen and present suitable artists. These professionals have usually worked with several different artists in the past and are happy to make recommendations. Many architects who specialize in church architecture are now supplying a team of artisans to install art in new buildings. This arrangement can often be of great benefit to client and artist alike. The committee has to be careful to challenge the professional team to design for its particular parish and not simply fall back on a typical "package" design.

How much do stained glass windows cost?

In stained glass, as with any building addition, you get what you pay for. A leaded glass window constructed of inexpensive cathedral glass in a simple, unpainted design will cost a great deal less than a window of the same size that uses handmade glass and incorporates figures, etching and silver staining. The reasons for the difference have to do with material costs and fabrication time, among other things.

First, the difference in material costs is substantial; handmade (antique) glass is almost five times as expensive as machine-made glass (visually, of course, there is no comparison between the two). Fabrication time needed to perform glass treatments, such as painting, etching and silver staining, is another important factor. This type of work can triple the time (and hence the labor costs) needed to make the window. Added to this are the equipment costs for studios that create work with painted, etched and silver stained glass. To do this work, they need kilns, etching and sandblasting booths, as well as highly skilled workers to perform these techniques.

The committee can get an idea of the approximate cost of the window by contacting three or four stained glass studios and asking for a price range based on the square footage of the window. In doing this, the researcher should make it clear that the window is for a church. By matching this information with research on the type of window the church wants, the committee can establish a reasonable estimate of the cost of the window. In dealing with the artist, the committee can choose either to set this figure as the budget for the window, or it can solicit bids from artists and use the estimate as a baseline against which to gauge the bids.

How does a parish typically raise money to pay for stained glass windows?

An important job for many committees is to gather funds and make sure that the project will fit the available budget. The committee can elect to find individual donors or to solicit donations from the entire community. Committee members will have varying levels of experience in fundraising; having an experienced fundraiser or publicist on the committee is a bonus. The good news is that stained glass is a popular addition to a church, and people are often happy to contribute to its creation.

One way to ease money pressures is to schedule the project to be completed in various stages, each stage with its own budget, so that costs are spread out over time. Another strategy that can make fundraising process easier is dividing the project into sections of varying size, so that people wishing to donate have several contribution levels to choose from.

What role should the donors play in decision-making?
This is always a delicate issue. It is important to remember that the goal of the church is to commission works of art that will enhance the place for liturgy over the long term. To do this, committee members and donors need to see beyond their personal tastes to what is best for the worship environment and most suitable to the style of architecture and needs of the space. It is generally best if the committee can make these decisions in advance and then open the possibilities to donors.

If a donor insists on taking over the process or makes unreasonable demands, the committee should seriously consider turning down the donation. While this is difficult to do, the gift of an unsuitable window is not a favor to the church, and the committee should be able to find other funding sources.

Memorial gifts are another tricky issue, as there are strong sensitivities concerning proper commemoration of the dead ("What would she have liked?"). Again, the committee needs to stick to its plan unless there is a good reason to change it. The conditions of a memorial gift or donation should never compromise the future mission of the parish.

How does the committee determine which style of window is appropriate to its church building?
This part of the process can be hard work for committees. Members may be united by the idea that an artwork is needed, but when they begin to discuss what they want, they may find that their respective visions of the work — style, subject, and so on — don't agree. The presence of older stained glass in the space can complicate things further, leading to debates over whether it is better to follow the previous windows' style (even to the point of hiring the same company!) or go in a new direction.

A good way to establish a sense of direction is to create a list of characteristics that enhance the space and reflect the values and spiritual journey of the congregation. The committee and artists then have a starting point and sense of direction. Deciding the purpose of the window is an important part of the process. In discussing the role of the window — for example, to block or attenuate the light, to take emphasis off of an uninspiring view, to convey a message — the committee can see how much common ground exists and can then move ahead more easily.

The lists of characteristics below came from three different committees and reflect the varying needs and buildings of different communities. Even though they are different, each list is a sufficient starting point for a design.

Committee A
• transparent look, idea of light, non-domineering
• large, light areas without strong patterns
• some realistic elements, but no dominant feature
• simple backgrounds, not cluttered or oppressive
• tending toward modern, abstract style with peaceful quality
• unifying color scheme or other unifying element
• artistic originality — some reflection of our Latvian heritage
• dislike: painted faces, extreme realism, busy clutter

Committee B
• strong, dramatic figures
• artistic originality and expressive faces
• warm, rich colors
• visual expression of our historic mission to native peoples
• painted details
• block exterior views and modulate light
• dislike: weak colors, weak figures

Committee C
• gentle, protective and rhythmic forms
• suggestive of plants, waves, environment
• evoke spiritual atmosphere without specific symbols
• delicate, quiet colors — transparent or translucent glass
• three elements: earth, human and spiritual
• dislike: primary colors, realism, stereotypical symbols

Committee A was from a parish with an older church building that had almost twenty clear windows — most of them quite high — surrounding the assembly. It is obvious that the intention was not to have "teaching windows," but rather to create windows that convey peace and unity, as well as give the church a beautiful, light-filled environment for worship. The church had been raising money for a few years and chose one artist to create all of the windows.

Committee B had a new building and a teaching mission. The windows were a strong focal point behind the altar and had a second purpose of blocking the bright eastern light. These windows were also seen as a message to the wider community and visitors about the heritage and continuing vision of the parish. The monumental architecture and dark interior suited the style of windows commissioned, and the rich, warm colors fostered the sense of mystery desired.

Committee C was from a chapel located in a chronic care hospital. Here, the emphasis was on quiet, healing environments and colors. The artwork that went into this space was a free-standing screen in front of, and visually connected to, a large clear window that looked out onto a beautiful forest.

Direction from the committee is important and useful, but if the artist is to produce creative and original work, that direction has to leave room for inspiration. It isn't necessary, or even helpful, for the committee to decide what the details of the window will be; this is the artist's responsibility. Instead, general guidance such as that given in the sample lists above is ideal. If members keep an open mind and use such lists as guides, it is likely that they will find an artist whose work appeals to most of them. In other words, the committee has to select an artist it can trust.

Who directs the work?

The main elements of a stained glass project are design, fabrication and installation. The usual role of the committee, after choosing the artist, is to work with the artist as the design is being developed. The committee chairperson usually acts as the designated contact person between artist and committee. Once fabrication is underway, the artist deals more with the institution's administration (or the architect and contractor, if the building is new) to schedule visits, arrange for payment and coordinate the installation. In the initial negotiations with the artist the committee should make sure the roles of all interested parties are defined in writing. This reduces the chance of problems later on.

Choosing an Artist

"To Do" List

1. Create a list of questions for artists. Some examples: What is your mission as a stained glass artist? How do you see the committee having input into the design? What is your current schedule like?
2. Send out letters to artists with possible interview times or a competition schedule.
3. Interview artists.
4. Send written confirmation to the chosen artist(s) and letters of thanks to the others (return their materials at the same time).
5. Inform the wider community of the decision.

QUESTIONS AND ANSWERS

Should the committee use a local artist?

A committee commissioning a window should be aware of what artists are available, both within and outside of its area. If there is a talented local artist the committee is comfortable with, then by all means it should use him or her! If there are few local artists, or the range of available styles is too narrow, the committee should look further afield.

When an artist's studio is some distance from the church building, there are some understandable concerns about how the committee can view the work in progress, and whether the artist will be as understanding and responsive as a local artist.

There are many ways to keep in touch, including telephone, fax and e-mail. These work as well across continents as they do across town. A studio visit requires a bit more time and energy, although photographs of the work in progress can be arranged. Generally, if the committee has hired an experienced, reliable artist, the work and scheduling will go smoothly.

The artist's ability to understand the committee's needs is really not a matter of geography. Many artists work nationally and internationally. The breadth of a search for an artist should depend upon the size of the commission and the schedule. A committee commissioning larger works that have a set schedule (for example, the opening of a new church building) can afford to look beyond its local area. If the commission is small, or will be done over a period of several years, it is usually better to work locally.

What should a committee expect from a preliminary presentation?

An artist will usually present slides of previous work, describe his or her approach to design, and answer the committee's questions. Members will want to share with the artist the desired characteristics of the work, timetable, budget limitations and a sense of the vision of the wider community. In the presentation it is important that the artist take some time to describe his or her training, techniques and work process.

Can the committee request free preliminary designs?

Designing stained glass for a church is a complex process, drawing as it does on all of the artist's creative capacity. The design work is in many ways the hardest, the most important and the most undervalued part of the process. The finest craft in the world is all for naught without a worthy design to build on. A good design takes time to produce, and an artist designing original work for a specific building should be compensated accordingly. If the committee wishes to have a number of designs to choose from, then it should consider holding a competition rather than relying on artist interviews. In fairness to the artists, however, the parish should pay for all of the designs that it commissions.

What about a young artist, or an artist with a slim portfolio?
References and an impressive selection of previous work increase a committee's confidence, and it is customary to expect this from a professional artist. Of course, a young artist who has not done many commissions does not have much work to draw upon, making it harder to get commissions and locking the artist into a vicious circle that perpetuates his or her inexperience. There are two situations in which a newcomer would be most likely to work out: a small project, or one in which the artist works with an established fabrication studio to create and install the work. Everyone needs to start somewhere, and the committee may want to seize the chance to help launch a great career.

What if the committee doesn't find anything it likes in the previous works of artists?
Sometimes a committee is looking for the exact work that will fit its space, and members are disappointed when they don't find it among any of the presented works. Most likely the committee will not see a window that perfectly suits its church building because *that* window hasn't been created yet!

When viewing previous work, the committee should look to see whether an artist has created windows appropriate to previous settings and clients. The members should ask the artist how his or her work responded to various settings and addressed the client's requirements. Previous designs are just an indication of direction and capability; what the committee is really choosing is an artist with the talent to do good work, as well as the sensitivity and flexibility to do the best work for their particular situation and church.

Is it important that the artist be of the same faith as the commissioning community?
While an artist of the same faith may start with a built-in understanding of the religion, there is no guarantee that his or her artistic expression of it will be what the committee wants. It is reasonable to expect that the artist will be sensitive and respectful of the liturgical tradition of the particular church. The artist will probably also need further study and guidance as he or she prepares to design. Nevertheless, some wonderful windows and imagery have arisen from an artist who brought new eyes to a client's faith. The committee's first priority is to find an artist whose work it appreciates and with whom wants to work.

What is the best way to inform the parish about the committee's choice of artist?
One of the most positive and enjoyable ways for the committee to share its decision with the parish is to arrange for the chosen artist to give a

presentation. The presentation could be set within the context of a reflection on the nature of light and color, and the medium of stained glass. The artist can introduce his or her work process, show slides of previous projects and explain the techniques used. This meeting often generates interest and excitement about the project, and it is best if this presentation is open to anyone who wishes to attend. This is a good time for the artist to interact with and meet parishioners before the design process begins. When the design is complete and has been approved by the committee, the artist can make another presentation.

What if parishioners take advantage of this opportunity and tell the artist — in no uncertain terms — how they want the window to look?

Creating a commissioned piece of art is a delicate tightrope for an artist to walk. It involves careful listening to all of the various (and often conflicting) needs and ideas being expressed. Through careful discernment, the artist can find the fundamental values and qualities that need to be expressed in the work. The committee can be of great value here in expressing who the parish is as a community celebrating the liturgy and the kind of qualities (rather than specific images) they wish to find in the work.

Although it is a sensitive point, it is unlikely that every person in the parish will be pleased with the window. It is not possible to create a work of art that reflects the taste of every individual. Thankfully, the committee's job is not to find art that pleases everybody; that is the difference between this task and choosing a work of art for someone's home, for example. The committee needs to take a broader, long-term view and then commission work that suits the church building, creates a fitting place for the celebration of the liturgy, and addresses the parish's spiritual life. When the parish understands the committee's work, many illusions are dispelled, and respect is accorded to its decisions.

What if there is an artist in the parish who would like to make and/or donate the window? How should the committee handle this?

With care! Perhaps you have a talented professional stained glass artist in your community. Consider yourself lucky! Welcome his or her contribution, or engage the artist for the commission. If the artist is an amateur, however, caution is in order. The reason for this is simple: Stained glass windows are meant to be a long-lasting contribution to the architectural fabric of the church. They should be well designed and crafted. Windows made by hobbyists often stand out in a church — and not in a positive way.

The professional will be knowledgeable about window structure, support, framing, ventilation and the prevention of condensation. More importantly, a professional artist generally has more experience designing for a variety of sites and is more likely to produce a design that is appropriate to the church.

The committee should seriously consider a proposal from a parishioner, make its decision, and then communicate it clearly. Misunderstandings happen easily, and it is very difficult to undo the damage they can cause.

What are the rules for running a competition?
There are no set rules for a competition, although there are some conventions that should be followed. In a competition, it is important that the committee be well-organized, deal fairly with all of the competitors, and maintain communication so that artists are not kept in the dark unnecessarily.

The following is a brief outline of the steps in a design competition.

- Publish a call for entries describing your project; create a short list of two to five artists based on initial slide submissions.
- Appoint a jury that includes experts in art, liturgy and architecture, as well as representatives of the parish at large.
- Create a package for each artist with architectural drawings, a list of desired characteristics or possible themes for the windows, a copy of the mission statement, the schedule and budget for the window, the competition schedule and information on design fees. (In 1999 the customary design fee for each artist in a competition ranged from $1000 for a single window to $5000 for a series of windows.)
- Set a time for interviews with the architect and a site tour for each participant.
- Arrange a time and place for artists to meet representatives of the committee and discuss any questions concerning the project.

The design time for the competition may be between six and twelve weeks, depending on the size of the project. Early in the process, the committee should arrange firm timeslots for each artist to present his or her design. At the time of the presentation, if not sooner, artists should be told when the decision will be made. The committee should stick to this date and inform both successful and unsuccessful candidates at that time.

At the end of the competition, the committee should ensure that all designs, models and samples are returned to the contestants.

Design and Fabrication

Questions and Answers
What is the task of the committee once it has chosen an artist?
Once the committee has chosen an artist, its role in the commissioning process changes somewhat. During the design process, it is helpful if either

the chairman or another designated member can act as a sounding board for the artist's ideas and directions. The pastor or another minister on the staff can be very helpful at this stage in contributing to discussions concerning the theological aspects of the work.

How much direction should the committee or designated person give the artist during the design process?
Committees sometimes feel they are being helpful by giving the artist pictures of what they would like to see in the windows and a detailed description of symbols, colors and images. There are certainly studios that prefer to copy a picture (or a window it has made before) rather than create an original design. This is an uninspired approach, and clients should not suggest it or be willing to settle for it.

Artists don't create new designs in a vacuum, however, and input is essential. The artist should be invited to attend the liturgy, or perhaps a building committee meeting or a social event, to allow her or him to learn about the community in an informal way. The qualities and characteristics desired for the windows should be known and respected by the artist.

Who decides on themes for the windows?
Themes for the windows can come as a direction from the committee and may take the form of a *plan of iconography*. Sometimes the artist has the artistic and theological knowledge to create such a plan and may prefer autonomy. Alternatively, iconography can be worked out in concert with the committee. Not all artists — or committees — have the knowledge and experience necessary to create a plan of iconography, and the parish may want to consult an outside resource person for this work.

Can various donors be allowed to decide on themes for the windows?
No. Allowing the donor's favorite subject, image or saint to determine iconography does not establish meaningful content in stained glass windows. In cases where there is a single window or many existing windows, however, the donor's ideas may be considered by the committee in light of what else is near the donated window.

Can the committee take the artist's designs to another studio that is willing to do the work for a better price?
No. This is quite unethical. In addition, a studio that is willing to undercut an artist while appropriating his or her design is not likely to produce good work. Translating a sketch into stained glass calls for artistry and vision. A studio that quotes a low price will probably be using cheap glass and cutting corners everywhere it can, since it has no real investment of time or

pride in the window. The end product will have little beauty or integrity and will be quite unworthy of gracing a church. It is better to establish a budget, or at least a range of costs, that everyone deems fair before the process is too far along.

What other resource persons will the artist need?
The artist will need to work with the architect or a liturgical consultant, especially if the building is under construction. Before designing, he or she will need drawings, dimensions and material samples. As design work nears completion, the artist and architect will need to consult on framing and installation specifications.

What factors does the artist take into account when designing a window or series of windows?
An artist takes many factors into account when she or he designs: the style of architecture, how light works in the building, and the surrounding materials, textures and colors. Some artists make a three-dimensional model of the church to help them visualize the space and the passage of light throughout the day. This is particularly useful if the church is still under construction.

The needs of the liturgy, the themes and theology to be expressed, and the qualities desired by the committee are also important. Budget restrictions, technical challenges and integration with the other windows need to be considered as well.

All of these considerations are merely groundwork. When an artist begins the design process, something else happens: The creative act of drawing takes on a life of its own and leads to new ideas and images. These inspirations are like gems, and they are found not by mere imaginings or analysis but through the whole creative process. It is a marvelously transcendent experience — a spiritual connection.

As the design nears completion, the artist begins to develop it into a format suitable for presentation. The challenge here is to try to create on paper what the window will look like when it is installed. Only glass really looks like glass, of course, but with a mix of materials and media, it is possible to achieve a reasonable presentation of how a window will look. The inclusion of glass samples in the presentation that accompanies the design can help committee members visualize the window.

How much should the design work cost?
Generally, design work is ten to fifteen percent of the overall cost of the project, unless this has been paid through a competition fee.

Can the committee ask the artist for a written proposal as well?
Certainly. Artists generally provide a written proposal along with design work. The committee may ask the artist to include concepts, themes and design approaches; location and dimensions of each piece; techniques and materials; work and fee schedules; framing specifications; installation requirements; and lighting and maintenance requirements.

Should the parish have a contract with the artist?
When commissioning a work of art, it is always wise to have a contract or letter of agreement laying out the above points with the artist.

After the artist has completed the design, can the committee ask for changes?
Most artists are willing to make some design changes, but it is a delicate issue. The elements of a stained glass window design are interconnected — this line leading to that color, forming the edge of that image — and it is difficult to change one aspect of the work without making several other changes. Like surgery, design changes should be done only for a good reason, and they should result in an overall improvement. If the committee is changing previously agreed-upon concepts, they should be prepared to compensate the artist for the additional time needed to make the changes.

What if the artist makes changes to the work during the fabrication process?
Creating a window is an organic and artistic process — not a simple process of manufacture. In the process of fabrication, the artist is translating a sketch into glass. In the scaling up and realization of the work, there is sometimes a need to adjust the cartoons and the glass treatments to improve the proportions, coloration and "flow" of the window. The client will need to trust the artist in the creation of the work and understand that he or she wants to create the best possible window from the design. The client should be informed of any major changes in the artwork and the reasons for it, and be given an opportunity to respond.

Can the members of the committee visit the studio while the window is being made?
This will be up to the individual artist. A studio visit to see the work in progress is an enjoyable and exciting event, especially when the whole committee can be present at the same time to listen to the artist explain the process of creating stained glass, watch the glass being cut, and perhaps try their hands at glass painting. Firsthand knowledge of how windows are made is certainly better than trying to visualize it from descriptions!

Installation and Celebration

"TO DO" LIST

1. Find out when the installation of the windows will be complete.

2. Consider creating a pamphlet or guide sheet to the windows, or if a booklet on the new building is being made, make sure to include information about the windows. Check with the artist about permission to use design drawings. (See page 91.)

3. If the windows are part of a new building, they most likely will be dedicated with the building as a whole. The committee should do some research into its church's tradition: Is there a ritual or a prayer for blessing stained glass windows? (In the Roman Catholic tradition, for example, windows are dedicated when the building is dedicated. However, the 1989 *Book of Blessings* also has an "Order for the Blessing of Articles for Liturgical Use." This order could be used when windows are added to an already-dedicated building, or even as an additional rite after the building is dedicated, to draw attention to the new work.)

4. Consider scheduling tours in which members of the committee are available after Sunday liturgies to show parishioners the new windows and encourage people to gaze at them, react to them, and then hear a little about them.

5. Consider inviting the artist to come (when and if this is feasible) and speak to the assembly.

6. Consider contacting the local media and inviting them to publicize the new work. (This may help with fundraising.)

7. Decide upon a method of archiving all materials concerning the project.

QUESTIONS AND ANSWERS

Who is responsible for the delivery of the stained glass to the church?
The artist should make these arrangements.

Who installs the windows?
The artist, along with an experienced installation team, usually has this responsibility. The artist, in consultation with the architect, will have finalized the installation methods and framing details during the design and fabrication period. Coordination with the site supervisor of a building under construction is essential. Arriving with stained glass windows and scaffolding while the stone floor is being laid does not make for an efficient installation. Having a site supervisor who is both good at scheduling and helpful to outside contractors is a blessing.

Are there any special technical considerations when installing stained glass windows?
The most significant threat to stained glass windows is the possibility of thermal breakage, which occurs when windows are placed too close to a thermopane. (There should be a one-inch space between the outer glass and a stained glass panel.) The other major problem is poor ventilation between the exterior (usually clear) glass and the leaded stained glass window. Condensation that occurs between these layers of glass can be eliminated with adequate ventilation. These technical factors are part of the artist's or studio's responsibilities and should be planned in conjunction with the architect to ensure a well designed, problem-free installation.

Who pays for the scaffolding?
Usually the client pays for the scaffolding, lift or other rental equipment used during installation. This should be covered in the contract or letter of agreement.

Who pays for insurance on the project?
While the project is in the studio, it is generally the artist's responsibility to insure it. The artist should also cover insurance during transport. Once the stained glass arrives at the client's site, it comes under the building's insurance policy. The church's insurance company should be notified of the new windows.

Who is responsible for cleaning the exterior windows and the framing that holds the windows?
The client should arrange to have the exterior clear glass windows cleaned inside and out before the stained glass is installed. The window framing in a building under construction is sometimes covered with plaster and paint, and the window installation should wait until there is a clean, safe environment.

If the windows are installed when there is still considerable construction to be done, the chances of damage are very high. A construction site is no place for stained glass windows, and their installation should be scheduled as late as possible in the building process. If an earlier installation is necessary, the windows should be protected with plywood.

What can the committee expect in terms of a warranty on craftsmanship?
Any issues pertaining to warranty must be specified in the contract between the artist and the commissioning parish. While it isn't usually difficult to guarantee that a leaded stained glass window will stand the test of time, there is no way of guaranteeing that someone will not break a piece of glass — or a

whole window — either by accident or through vandalism. Glass can break; fortunately, windows can also be repaired.

An additional concern is the framing system that holds the stained glass in place. The framing system itself can put pressure on stained glass and cause cracking. The framing system should be approved by the artist before a guarantee is given.

If a window contains a very rare glass or a difficult-to-match color and is in a position where breakage may occur (such as ground level), it may be worthwhile for the client to purchase a small amount of spare glass. This will come in handy in the event that repairs are needed.

Who owns the copyright on the work?
The artist owns the copyright to the work unless a contract transfers copyright in whole or in part to another party.

Can the parish make cards and posters of the work for sale?
If the parish does not own the rights to the windows, it must request permission from the copyright owner to make cards, posters or other reproductions of the image for sale. Many artists will welcome this opportunity to have their work seen by a wider audience.

Should the committee arrange publicity for the artist and windows after installation?
By all means — especially with a large commission. The publicity and public interest will bring visitors and possibly new members to the church. Enjoy and celebrate the new work in your church!

Should the parish formally dedicate the windows?
Usually there is some form of dedication of the windows when the assembly is gathered. The parish may want to invite the artist to speak during the liturgy or at a reception afterwards. Donors and committee members should also be present and acknowledged during the dedication ceremony.

APPENDIX I:
MAINTENANCE AND RESTORATION

This book is about commissioning new windows and working with artists; however, some short note about the care and restoration of windows is in order.

CARE

Maintaining leaded glass is simple. Windows should be washed with distilled water and vinegar. Annual dusting with a soft cloth is advisable. No harsh chemicals or abrasives should ever be used on stained glass windows. Sandblasted glass, which tends to attract dust and fingerprints, can be protected with a product called "Glass Armor." Consult your stained glass studio about this treatment.

RESTORATION

By the thirteenth century, stained glass studios were busy repairing and maintaining windows from the twelfth century! Most people are surprised that the stained glass windows of Europe's cathedrals have been out of their frames and in the studio almost once a century — at the very least for re-leading, if not for repairs to the glass itself. Very simply, the lead, which must be soft and malleable enough to wrap around tiny, complex shapes of glass, deteriorates. Although it generally does not break, glass is vulnerable to storms, vandalism and accidents, and it may need replacement or restoration. (Medieval glass is softer than present-day handmade glass, however, and is effected by acid rain and pollution, which deteriorates it.)

Many studios specialize in repairs and restoration, and the best way of addressing the condition of a window is for the architect or designated supervisor to call the Stained Glass Association of America (see Appendix II) and ask for the names of local or regional studios that specialize in restoration. These studios can provide information on the condition of a church's windows and a program and schedule for restoration.

APPENDIX II: RESOURCES

Where can a parish find stained glass artists? Where can it find further information about what has been covered in this book? There are many people to consult and places to look! These include:

- The church's architect
- Liturgical or art consultant
- Local arts and crafts guilds, which often have a resource center and/or slide library
- Local art galleries, which can provide the names of talented stained glass artists in the area
- Internet search engines, which can find samples of work by stained glass artists throughout the world.
- Print resources

E & A Letter
Liturgy Training Publications
1800 North Hermitage Avenue
Chicago IL 60622-1101
1-800-933-1800   fax 1-800-933-7094
orders@ltp.org   www.ltp.org
> *This monthly magazine has an artists' portfolio page each month on the inside front cover that regularly includes stained glass artists, as well as occasional articles on particular installations.*

Faith and Form
PO Box 51307
Durham NC 27717-1307
Attention: Barbara Hilliard
> *This quarterly publication of the Interfaith Forum on Religion, Art and Architecture, a special interest group of the American Institute of Architects, has an Artist/Artisan Directory at the back.*

The Guild Resource Book
931 East Main Street #106
Madison WI 53703-2955
1-800-969-1555   fax 1-608-256-1938
> *Request the volume on architectural arts, which includes stained glass and liturgical artists.*

Stained Glass Magazine
6 SW 2nd Street, Suite #7
Lee's Summit MO 64063-2352
1-800-438-9581
> *This is a magazine for stained glass artists, but a subscription for the parish will help educate a committee and familiarize its members with the art form from the artist's perspective.*

Ministry and Liturgy
160 East Virginia Street #290
San Jose CA 95112-5876
1-408-286-8505   fax 1-408-287-8748
> *This magazine has listings of artists and artisans, and sponsors an annual competition, often awarding prizes to recent stained glass installations.*

Glass Art Magazine
PO Box 260377
Highlands Ranch CO 80163-0377
1-303-791-8998   fax 1-303-791-7739
> *This magazine offers articles and photographs of current stained glass projects.*

• Workshops

Form/Reform Conference
Conference Services
PO Box 5226
Rockford IL 61125
> *This national conference on church architecture and art, held every 18 months in a different location, gathers artists, architects and parishioners. Studios and artists exhibit their work and offer presentations.*

Interfaith Forum on Religion, Art and Architecture
> *As a special interest group of the American Institute of Architects, IFRAA has both national and regional meetings. The best way to stay apprised of these meetings is to subscribe to* Faith & Form *(see above).*

APPENDIX III: GLOSSARY

Words italicized in the main body of the book are defined below.

acid-etching. The process of removing a thin top layer of color on flashed glass. This technique uses hydrofluoric acid, which dissolves the surface layer of the glass and creates a series of gradated tones and sharp contrasts that reveal the underlying base color.

American opalescent. A rolled glass made of mixed colors on a translucent white base, first invented by Louis Comfort Tiffany in the 1870s.

annealing. The final cooling process in the manufacture of sheet glass.

antique glass. Handmade blown glass made using the medieval method, featuring many textures, striations and bubbles. The word "antique" refers to the process rather than the age of the glass. This glass is made today chiefly in France and Germany.

appliqué. A technique using colorless epoxy resins or ultraviolet adhesives to glue colored glass, jewels, and so forth, to a base glass. This technique is sometimes used to achieve a sculptured, three-dimensional effect.

armature. A metal framework of geometric design that supports the stained glass panels within a window opening.

badger. A soft, wide brush of badger hair used in glass painting to spread or stipple a wash of glass paint.

bevels. Angles cut into the edges of glass that are then highly polished. Bevels can be hand- or machine-made.

brilliant-cutting. The process of grinding shapes into the surface of (usually clear) glass with a series of abrasive stones. Waterford crystal goblets are created this way.

came. The H-channel form that holds individual pieces of glass together, usually made of lead but also of zinc, brass or copper. The soft, malleable quality of lead came allows it to follow complex glass shapes. It is usually milled in six-foot lengths of varying widths.

cartoon. A full-size drawing on paper of a stained glass window. The cartoon may be color or black-and-white. It contains all the patterning for the lead and information for glass painting. Cartoons are often hand-drawn but may also be achieved through mechanical or photographic means. Commercial studios may reuse cartoons dozens of times by simply resizing the window or border shape.

carving. See **sandblasting.**

cathedral glass. An inexpensive, commercial machine-rolled colored glass available in various textures but with very limited colors.

copper foil. A technique of bonding pieces of glass together developed by Louis Comfort Tiffany in the nineteenth century that is still widely used for small decorative items and lampshades. It is achieved through the use of adhesive copper tape (foil) that encloses each piece of glass. The pieces are then bonded by soldering the entire surface of the piece. Copper foil provides a more irregular and sculpted line than lead but is not suited to architectural projects, as it lacks the strength and flexibility of lead came.

crown glass. Discs of blown glass that are spun into varying sizes and made in different colors. They have a small knob at the center where they were removed from the blow pipe. These rondels are also made by being cast or pressed into molds. Also known as bull's-eye or spun glass.

cutline. A tracing of the lead pattern from the cartoon onto translucent paper, which is then used as a template for cutting glass in English style. The cutline is placed on a light box, and the glass is placed over it to be cut.

dalle de verre. A technique using inch-thick colored slab or cast glass, shaped into pieces and faceted on the surface, and then set into concrete or epoxy resin. Although it was used extensively in the 1950s and '60s, its popularity has waned since that time.

design. The sketch or artwork for a window, often done at a 1:10 scale. The design is the basis for the full-size cartoon.

enamels. Various colored glass powders that can be mixed and used for painting on glass. Enamels are fired at a temperature of approximately 1100 degrees Fahrenheit (600 degrees Celsius) and have a translucent but rather dull appearance.

epoxy resin. A synthetic, colorless adhesive used either to hold colored glass onto a clear glass base, known as appliqué, or for setting glass in *dalle de verre.*

etching. See **acid-etching** or **sandblasting.**

faceted glass. See *dalle de verre.*

favrile glass. Iridescent glass created by exposing molten glass to metallic fumes and oxides, invented by Louis Comfort Tiffany in the 1880s. It has a silky, smooth quality and helped make Tiffany's art glass and lamps exceptionally popular. "Favrile" is Latin for "fabricated."

fenestration. The arrangement of windows in a building.

firing. The process of heating painted or enameled pieces so that the paint, stain or enamel fuses permanently to the surface of the glass. Most enamels are fired at 1100 to 1250 degrees Fahrenheit (600 to 680 degrees Celsius).

flashed glass. Two-layered glass in which a top layer of a darker color is applied to a bottom layer of usually clear or light-colored glass.

float glass. Clear glass created by floating molten glass on liquid tin. This produces perfectly regular transparent window glass.

full size. The measurement of a window opening to the farthest point occupied by the glass.

fusing. The process of kiln-firing multiple pieces of individual glass at a temperature of 1400 degrees Fahrenheit (760 degrees Celsius) in which the pieces melt and remain bonded to each other or a sheet of base glass. Special glasses that have similar coefficients of expansion and contraction are used for this process.

glass. A super-cooled liquid with no crystalline structure and varying composition, primarily silica sand with soda or potash and lime, which is added to facilitate a lower melting temperature. The color in glass is created with metallic oxides that are dissolved into the molten glass.

glass paint. A glass treatment composed of brown or black iron oxide and finely ground glass, used to give added detail, linework and shading to glass. It is permanently fused to the glass through kiln-firing at a temperature between 1200 and 1250 degrees Fahrenheit (650 to 680 degrees Celsius).

glazier. A person whose work is cutting glass, leading it up, and setting it into windows.

grisaille. From the French *grisailler,* "to paint grey," decorative leaded windows of clear, white or pale-tinted glass that may be unpainted or painted with a repetitive foliage motif or ornamental geometric design.

grozing. Trimming away the edge of a piece of glass into its desired shape.

halation. Phenomenon whereby light-colored glass surrounded by darkness produces a blurred effect in which the light seems to spread beyond the boundaries of the glass.

handblown glass. Glass made by a person or team using a blow pipe and shaping tools. See **antique glass.**

lamented glass. Glass of two or more layers bonded together with a resin. It is most often used as a safety glass since it is fairly resistant to breakage and shattering.

lathekin. A small tool of wood or bone used to open and straighten lead cames.

lead. See **came.**

lehr. A long oven in which glass is annealed as it travels along a continuous belt.

lenses. Circular cast optical glass — usually clear — made in various sizes with different depths and incorporated into stained glass windows as a decorative, dimensional feature.

lusters. Iridescent metallic colors painted and fired onto the surface of glass.

matte painting. Tonal shading on glass that is usually fired on after the trace painting has been applied. It further controls the light by creating a modeled, three-dimensional effect.

mullions. Vertical bars that divide a window into sections.

opak. Clear or colored antique glass that has been flashed with an opaque white layer.

opal. Clear or colored antique glass that has been flashed with a transparent layer, giving it a pearl-like quality.

opalescent. See **American opalescent.**

panel. A single element in a stained glass window that is not usually larger than 40 inches by 40 inches. The shape of the panel depends on the window design and whether or not it is a tracery panel. Larger panels require support bars.

pattern. The full-size paper template made from the cartoon, around which the glass is cut out. There may be hundreds or thousands of patterns in a large stained glass window. Continental-style cutting is done using paper patterns that are placed on top of the glass and then cut around.

plan of iconography. A comprehensive plan for the subject matter of an entire fenestration.

plating. The sandwiching of two individual pieces of glass within one lead came. Occasionally, a separate piece of glass is soldered onto the back with its own lead border — usually as an onsite repair.

prism. A piece of triangular clear glass that casts a spectrum of colors as light passes through it. Prisms are occasionally incorporated into windows to create a dimensional and ornamental effect.

quarry. A pattern of diamond-shaped or square panes of glass used in grisaille windows or as a background for figures.

reamy glass. A type of antique glass with a wavy, flowing texture produced by mixing molten glass of different hardnesses. Also known as Danziger glass.

resist. A material used to protect various areas of glass during acid-etching and sandblasting.

reverse painting. Painting done with oils or acrylic on the back of glass using a sandblasted surface that will hold the pigments.

rolled glass. Glass that is manufactured by passing it through two parallel rollers. The rollers often create regular textures on the top surface. Cathedral and American opalescent glass is made this way, as is clear textured "industrial" glass.

rondel. A circular panel of leaded glass that is independent of its architectural setting.

rose window. A large circular window divided by tracery that radiates in petal-like or geometric shapes.

sandblasting. A glass treatment in which sand is propelled onto the surface of a piece of glass by compressed air, abrading the surface of the glass. Light sandblasting on clear glass, or etching, produces a frosted appearance. Sandblasting can also be used to cut very deeply into the glass to create a sculptural quality known as carving. Sandblasting is also used to remove the surface of flashed glass.

seedy glass. A type of antique glass with randomly scattered bubbles of varying sizes. A commercial version of this glass is made in rolled glass.

semi-antique glass. Glass manufactured through a "drawn" process that leaves striations. It seems reminiscent of antique glass, although it is not handblown and does not possess antique glass's irregular coloration and variations in thickness. Also called new antique, semi-antique comes in a very limited range of colors and is relatively inexpensive.

sight size. Also known as opening size, the measurement visible to the eye of the daylight opening of a window.

silver stain. A glass treatment in which silver nitrate is painted onto glass and fired at a low temperature. Silver stain penetrates the glass, giving it a permanent, transparent coloration ranging from pale yellow to deep amber. Introduced in the fourteenth century, it has remained a popular technique.

slab glass. Inch-thick cast glass used for making *dalle de verre* type windows.

slumping. The process of kiln forming or bending glass on a mold at temperatures of over 1200 degrees Fahrenheit (650 degrees Celsius).

soldering. The process by which the leads of a stained glass panel are bonded together. Wire solder is melted over all the joints of lead came on both sides of the panel.

spun glass. See **crown glass.**

streaky glass. A type of antique glass in which different colors or varying tones of one color are mixed while still molten, resulting in a sheet of glass with ribbons of color throughout.

support bar. A flat steel bar that is soldered to a glass panel, or a round iron bar that is attached to a leaded panel with copper ties. A support bar provides additional strength to a stained glass window and prevents it from bowing.

tee bar. T-shaped steel bar that is secured to a window frame on each side for support and onto which the stained glass panel is placed.

tempered glass. A type of safety glass made by heating the glass and then rapidly cooling it, which results in a tough glass that breaks into small pieces when shattered.

template. See **pattern.**

Tiffany glass. A type of rolled glass. See **American opalescent** and **favrile glass.**

trace painting. Usually the first painting on a piece of glass that is fired at a temperature between 1200 and 1250 degrees Fahrenheit (650 to 680 degrees Celsius). It creates strong, simple dark lines or outlines, as distinct from matte painting.

tracery. Ornamental stone work above a Gothic window that forms the openings for the stained glass.

transom. Window opening above a door or a larger window.

zinc came. A type of very rigid came sometimes used as additional support in leaded windows or for geometric door panels.